TRAITORS, SPIES, AND SECRET AGENTS

*True Stories of the Men and Women
Who Fought America's Secret Civil War*

CHUCK WATSON

Traitors, Spies, and Secret Agents

True Stories of the Men and Women Who Fought America's Secret Civil War

Chuck Watson

Crazy Dog Publishing

Published by Crazy Dog Publishing LLC

ISBN (Paperback): 979-8-950354-01-4

ISBN (eBook): 979-8-950354-06-9

Cover imagery generated with AI assistance and designed by Chuck Watson

TABLE OF CONTENTS

UNION

The Detective and the President

Allan Pinkerton Builds America's First Secret Service

The telegram arrived in Philadelphia on February 21, 1861, and its contents were alarming enough that Allan Pinkerton read it twice before acting.

Norman Judd, a Chicago lawyer and close associate of President-elect Abraham Lincoln, had received word from Pinkerton's operatives that something was being planned in Baltimore — something specific, something credible, something that had moved beyond the realm of the angry letter and the drunken threat that had become a routine feature of Lincoln's existence since his election in November. Baltimore was a secessionist city in a border state, its streets loud with Southern sympathy and louder still with the particular fury of men who felt the election of a Republican president was an act of war against their way of life. Pinkerton's people had been working the city for weeks, infiltrating the social clubs and militia organizations where the most dangerous talk was happening, and what they had found was not talk.

It was a plan.

The plan, as Pinkerton's operatives had pieced it together from conversations in barrooms and drawing rooms across Baltimore, was straightforward in its conception and potentially lethal in its execution. Lincoln's published itinerary called for his presidential train to pass through Baltimore on February 23 — the city was an unavoidable stop on the route from Springfield, Illinois to Washington — where he was to transfer between train stations in an open carriage, exposed to the crowds that would line the streets. The conspirators intended to use that exposure. A group of men — their number and specific identities still being established by Pinkerton's network — planned to create a disturbance in the crowd, draw the police escort's attention, and use the confusion to get close enough to the President-elect to kill him.

Pinkerton had been in the intelligence business long enough to know the difference between a rumor and a threat. This was a threat.

Allan Pinkerton had not come to the intelligence business by a conventional route — but then, nothing about Pinkerton's life had been conventional.

He was born in Glasgow, Scotland in 1819, the son of a police sergeant, and raised in the Gorbals — one of the most impoverished and violent neighborhoods in a city that had no shortage of either. He trained as a cooper — a barrel maker — and became involved in the Chartist movement, the working-class political organization that was demanding democratic reform from a British government disinclined to provide it. When the Chartist movement was suppressed and arrest warrants were issued for some of its more prominent members, Pinkerton made the decision that would define the rest of his life: he got on a ship.

He arrived in North America in 1842, made his way to Illinois, and settled eventually in the small town of Dundee, northwest of Chicago, where he established himself as a cooper and became, almost accidentally, a detective. The story he told — and he told it often, in the self-promotional mode that would characterize his entire career — was that he stumbled upon a counterfeiting operation while cutting wood on a deserted island in the Fox River, reported it to the local sheriff, and helped make the arrests. The sheriff was impressed enough to ask for his help again. And again. By the mid-1840s Pinkerton was doing more detective work than barrel making.

In 1850 he founded the Pinkerton National Detective Agency in Chicago — the first private detective agency in the United States, operating under a logo of an open eye and the motto "We Never Sleep" that would become one of the most recognized commercial images in nineteenth century America. The agency's early work was primarily railroad cases — the railroads were the most lucrative clients, their exposure to theft and fraud enormous as they expanded across the continent — but Pinkerton's methods and his reputation grew with his client list. He was not a subtle man, but he was a thorough one. His operatives were trained to observe, to cultivate sources, to maintain cover identities, and to gather information through the patient accumulation of detail rather than the dramatic confrontation. These were, in embryo, the methods of modern intelligence work.

He was also a committed abolitionist — his Dundee home had been a station on the Underground Railroad — and when the Southern states began seceding following Lincoln's election, Pinkerton's sympathies were entirely and aggressively with the Union.

The Baltimore Plot — as it would come to be known — was uncovered through the kind of patient undercover work that Pinkerton had been developing for a decade.

His operative, Harry Davies, had spent weeks cultivating a relationship with a Baltimore barber named Cypriano Ferrandini — a passionate Secessionist who had allegedly been organizing the conspiracy and who spoke freely to Davies once he was convinced of his sympathies. Ferrandini described the plan in terms that left little ambiguity about its seriousness: the attack on Lincoln during the carriage transfer between Baltimore's train stations, the deliberate creation of a disturbance to scatter the police escort, the use of the crowd's density as cover for the assassins.

What is not disputed is what Pinkerton did with the intelligence he had gathered. He contacted Norman Judd, presented his findings, and proposed a plan to move Lincoln through Baltimore secretly — bypassing the published itinerary entirely, traveling through the city on a night train that no one outside a small circle of trusted advisors would know about.

Lincoln was not immediately persuaded. He was uncomfortable with the idea of appearing to flee from a threat — a president who sneaked through a hostile city in the middle of the night was not the image he wanted to project in the fraught weeks before his inauguration. He had other sources of warning, including a report from General Winfield Scott and Secretary of State-designate William Seward's son Frederick, who arrived in Philadelphia on the same day as Pinkerton with similar intelligence gathered through different channels. The convergence of warnings from independent sources moved Lincoln from reluctance to agreement.

On the night of February 22, 1861, Abraham Lincoln boarded a sleeping car on the Philadelphia, Wilmington and Baltimore Railroad under conditions of elaborate secrecy. He was accompanied by Pinkerton and by Ward Hill Lamon, a large and physically formidable Illinois lawyer who served as Lincoln's informal bodyguard. Lincoln wore a soft felt hat rather than his distinctive stovepipe — a detail that would be savagely mocked in the press when it became known, caricaturists depicting him skulking through Baltimore in a Scottish cap and military cloak that bore no relation to what he actually wore but served the satirical purpose admirably.

The train passed through Baltimore in the early hours of February 23 without incident. Lincoln arrived in Washington safely. Whether the threat had been real enough to justify the elaborate precautions was debated immediately and has been debated ever since.

Pinkerton never doubted it.

In the weeks following Lincoln's inauguration, as the firing on Fort Sumter transformed political crisis into open war, Pinkerton found his path to the center of the Union's intelligence effort through the relationship that would define — and ultimately damage — his wartime career.

General George Brinton McClellan was one of the most celebrated soldiers in America in the spring of 1861. A West Point graduate who had served with distinction in the Mexican War and subsequently left the army for a successful career in railroad management, he was recalled to military service when the war began and given command of the Department of the Ohio — a position from which he conducted the small but successful western Virginia campaign that was the Union's first significant military success of the war. When the disaster at the First Battle of Bull Run in July 1861 revealed the catastrophic inadequacy of the Union's military preparation, Lincoln turned to McClellan to rebuild the army and restore confidence.

McClellan and Pinkerton had worked together before the war — Pinkerton's agency had done security work for the Illinois Central Railroad when McClellan was its vice president. The relationship was comfortable and mutually respectful. When McClellan needed someone to build an intelligence service for his newly designated Army of the Potomac, he turned to the man he knew.

Pinkerton accepted the assignment and set about building what would become the Union Intelligence Service — the first organized military intelligence operation in American history — with the same energy and methodological thoroughness he brought to everything he did. He established a network of agents operating in Confederate territory, developed procedures for the debriefing of escaped slaves and Confederate deserters, organized the systematic collection and analysis of captured documents, and created a reporting structure that brought intelligence from the field to army headquarters in a form that commanders could use.

It was, in many respects, a genuine achievement. The Union had entered the war with essentially no intelligence infrastructure — no trained agents, no established networks, no analytical capacity, no institutional knowledge of how to gather and process military intelligence. What Pinkerton built in the summer and autumn of 1861 was improvised, imperfect, and sometimes dangerously unreliable. It was also more than had existed before, and it established organizational precedents that would influence American military intelligence for decades.

The problem was not the organization. The problem was the numbers.

The systematic overestimation of Confederate troop strength that characterized Pinkerton's intelligence reporting to McClellan is one of the most consequential analytical failures in American military history, and understanding it requires understanding both what Pinkerton did wrong and why he did it.

Pinkerton's methodology for estimating Confederate strength was fundamentally sound in its design and catastrophically flawed in its execution. He gathered reports from multiple sources — agents in Confederate territory, escaped slaves and freedmen who had observed Confederate camps and movements, Confederate deserters, and captured documents. He attempted to cross-reference these reports to establish reliable figures. The approach was correct. The problem was in what happened to the numbers when they reached his desk.

Pinkerton consistently accepted the highest estimates from his sources and combined them in ways that compounded rather than corrected for error. When different sources gave different figures for the same unit, he tended to choose the larger number. When sources reported troops that could not be independently confirmed, he tended to include them rather than discount them. The result was a systematic inflation of Confederate strength that bore an increasingly tenuous relationship to reality.

The numbers he gave McClellan were not merely wrong. They were dramatically, persistently, and consequentially wrong. At various points during the Peninsula Campaign of 1862, Pinkerton estimated Confederate forces opposing McClellan at two to three times their actual strength. When McClellan had a genuine numerical advantage over Confederate General Joseph Johnston in the spring of 1862 — an advantage that a more aggressive commander might have used to end the war in Virginia before it fully developed — Pinkerton's estimates told him he was facing a superior force that could destroy his army if he moved incautiously.

McClellan, whose own temperamental disposition toward caution needed no encouragement, found in Pinkerton's estimates the intelligence justification for the delay and hesitation that drove Lincoln to distraction and his subordinates to fury. Every request for reinforcements, every refusal to advance, every elaborate preparation for a battle that was then postponed — McClellan could point to Pinkerton's numbers and say he was acting on the best available intelligence.

The relationship between Pinkerton and McClellan ended when McClellan's military career ended — which is to say, when Lincoln finally lost patience with the general's inaction and relieved him of command of the Army of the Potomac in November 1862, following his failure to pursue Lee's army aggressively after the Battle of Antietam.

Pinkerton did not stay to work with McClellan's successor. He returned to Chicago and his agency, taking with him the files he had accumulated during his time as intelligence chief and the unshakeable conviction that he had done his job well. He spent the rest of the war doing investigative work for the War Department — fraud cases, counterintelligence investigations, the kind of work his agency had always done

— and the postwar years rebuilding the Pinkerton Agency into the most powerful private detective organization in the country.

He wrote his memoirs in the 1870s and 1880s, producing a series of books that mixed genuine case histories with considerable embellishment, and that presented his Civil War intelligence work in the most favorable possible light. The Baltimore Plot became, in his telling, an unambiguous triumph — the conspiracy real, the danger absolute, the rescue of Lincoln from certain death a personal achievement of the first order. The intelligence failures of the Peninsula Campaign received considerably less attention.

History has been more balanced than Pinkerton was inclined to be about himself. The Baltimore Plot was real enough — some form of conspiracy existed, and moving Lincoln through the city secretly was a reasonable precaution given the intelligence available. The intelligence failures that fed McClellan's inaction were real too — and their consequences, measured in the lives of men who died in battles that a more aggressive Union commander might have prevented or shortened, were enormous.

Pinkerton was, in the end, exactly what his career suggested he was: a brilliant and innovative detective who had been given a job that was different in kind from anything he had done before, and who had performed parts of it with genuine skill and other parts with consequential inadequacy. He had built America's first organized military intelligence service from nothing, in the middle of a war, without a model to follow or a tradition to draw on. That was a real achievement.

He had also told the Union's most important general, repeatedly and systematically, that the enemy facing him was twice as strong as it actually was, and those miscalculations had helped prolong the bloodiest war in American history.

Both of these things were true. Both of them were Allan Pinkerton.

The Slaves Who Spied

Black Intelligence Networks and the Union War Effort

They moved through the Confederate world like ghosts — present everywhere, noticed by almost no one, carrying in their heads information that could change the course of a war.

The enslaved men and women of the Confederate South were, by the logic of the institution that owned them, invisible. They served at table while their enslavers discussed military strategy. They drove carriages that passed through Confederate fortifications. They dug the earthworks whose dimensions and locations they could measure with their eyes. They worked in the households of Confederate officers, the offices of Confederate officials, the hospitals where wounded Confederate soldiers described the battles they had survived. They were there for every conversation that the men who owned them considered private, because the men who owned them had long since stopped thinking of the people they enslaved as fully human — and people who are not fully human, in the logic of slavery, cannot really be listening.

They were listening.

The intelligence advantage this created for the Union Army was so obvious, so enormous, and so consistently underexploited that it stands as one of the great strategic failures of the Union war effort — and one of the great unacknowledged contributions to Union victory of the men and women who provided it anyway, through whatever channels were available to them, at whatever personal risk the provision required.

That risk was not theoretical. An enslaved person caught passing information to Union forces faced punishment that the law of the Confederate states left entirely to the discretion of the enslaver — which meant, in practice, that it could extend to death. The men and women who provided intelligence to Union forces did so in the full knowledge of what discovery would mean. They did it anyway, in numbers that the historical record — fragmentary, incomplete, and systematically biased toward the documentation of white experience — can only partially capture.

The first organized exploitation of what would come to be called "Black intelligence" in the Civil War happened almost by accident, at a Virginia peninsula fortification called Fort Monroe in the first weeks of the war.

Fort Monroe sat at the tip of the Virginia Peninsula — a Union-held installation in Confederate Virginia that became, almost immediately after the war began, a magnet for enslaved people attempting to reach Union lines. They came in ones and twos at first, then in larger groups — men and women who had calculated, with the practical intelligence of people whose survival had always depended on accurate assessment of their situation, that the arrival of Union forces in Virginia represented an opportunity that might not come again.

The legal status of these arrivals presented the Union Army with an immediate problem. The Fugitive Slave Act — still technically the law of the land — required the return of escaped enslaved people to their legal owners. Union officers were deeply divided about what to do. Many were not abolitionists. Many had no particular interest in the question of slavery one way or the other. They were soldiers, and the law was the law.

General Benjamin Butler was not a man who let the law get in the way of a useful solution. Butler was a Massachusetts lawyer and politician who had been given a military commission at the war's outset and who brought to his command the creative legal reasoning of a man who had spent his career finding ways around inconvenient obstacles. When three enslaved men arrived at Fort Monroe in May 1861 — having escaped from a Confederate labor detail that was building fortifications nearby — Butler declined to return them. His reasoning was elegant in its simplicity: since Virginia had declared itself in a state of rebellion against the United States, the laws of the United States, including the Fugitive Slave Act, did not apply in Virginia. And since the Confederate military was using enslaved labor to build fortifications against the Union, the enslaved people performing that labor were — by the laws of war — contraband of war, subject to seizure just like any other enemy military asset.

Contraband. The word spread through the enslaved population of the Virginia Peninsula with the speed of something long awaited. Within weeks, hundreds of people were arriving at Fort Monroe. Within months, thousands.

Butler was not, primarily, an intelligence officer. But he was a practical man, and the practical value of what was arriving at his gates was immediately apparent. These men and women had just come from Confederate Virginia. They had eyes. They had information. He began debriefing them.

What Butler's debriefings revealed — and what similar intelligence gathering operations at Union posts across the South would confirm over the following months and years — was that the enslaved population of the Confederacy constituted the most valuable and most underutilized intelligence asset in the entire war.

The information they carried was not abstract. It was specific, current, and operationally significant. An enslaved man who had spent the previous week helping to dig Confederate earthworks outside Yorktown could describe their location, their dimensions, their armament, and the number of men working on them with the precision of someone who had been there — because he had. A woman who had been working in the household of a Confederate officer could describe the conversations she had heard, the visitors who had come and gone, the papers she had seen on the desk when she cleaned the study. A group who had traveled by road from Richmond to the Peninsula could describe what they had observed along the route — troop concentrations, artillery positions, supply depots, the direction of military movement.

None of this intelligence required training to gather. It required only presence — which the enslaved population had in abundance — and the opportunity to transmit what had been observed to someone who could use it. Butler provided that opportunity at Fort Monroe. As the war expanded, Union commanders across the South began to understand and exploit the same resource — some systematically, some haphazardly, some not at all.

The failure to exploit it systematically was one of the Union war effort's most persistent and costly intelligence failures. The reasons were multiple and mutually reinforcing. Racism — the same assumption of Black invisibility that made enslaved people such effective intelligence gatherers — made many Union officers discount or ignore the information they received. The institutional structure of Union intelligence, such as it was, had been built around white agents operating in white social networks and was poorly designed to incorporate intelligence from a fundamentally different source. And the legal and political complexities surrounding the status of enslaved people in the early war — before the Emancipation Proclamation clarified the Union's position — made systematic exploitation of Black intelligence networks politically fraught in ways that had nothing to do with their operational value.

The intelligence came anyway — through whatever channels were available, exploited by whatever Union commanders were perceptive enough to recognize its value.

John Scobell's name appears in the historical record primarily through Allan Pinkerton's postwar memoirs — a source that requires careful handling given Pinkerton's well-documented tendency toward self-promotion and embellishment. With that caveat clearly stated, what Pinkerton describes is an intelligence operation of remarkable sophistication for its time.

Scobell, by Pinkerton's account, was a freed slave from Mississippi — educated, intelligent, and possessed of the particular combination of personal courage and social dexterity that deep cover intelligence work required. Pinkerton recruited him into his intelligence organization in late 1861, and Scobell subsequently conducted multiple operations inside Confederate territory — traveling through the Confederate South using his race as cover in a way that no white agent could have replicated.

The logic was brutally simple. A white man moving through Confederate territory without obvious military affiliation attracted scrutiny. An African American man moving through the same territory was, in the eyes of the Confederate social order, simply another Black person going about whatever business Black people went about — invisible by assumption, unworthy of serious attention. Scobell exploited this invisibility with systematic effectiveness, gathering intelligence about Confederate troop movements, fortifications, and supply arrangements that he transmitted back to Pinkerton's organization through a network of contacts that included members of a secret society called the Legal League — an organization of free Black people and escaped slaves who maintained communication networks across the Confederate South.

The historical record for Scobell's specific operations is thin — Pinkerton's memoirs are the primary source, and independent corroboration is limited. What can be said with confidence is that Pinkerton's organization did employ African American agents, that those agents operated inside Confederate territory, and that the intelligence they gathered contributed to Union operational planning during the Peninsula Campaign of 1862. The specific details of individual operations must be treated with appropriate caution given the limitations of the available sources.

What requires no caution is the acknowledgment of what those agents were doing and what it cost them to do it. A white Pinkerton operative captured behind Confederate lines faced imprisonment and potentially execution under the laws of war. An African American operative captured behind Confederate lines faced something considerably worse — the full weight of a system designed to reduce human beings to property, applied with the particular fury that the Confederate social order reserved for Black people who had stepped outside the boundaries it had drawn for them.

They operated anyway.

Harriet Tubman had already done the most dangerous thing imaginable before the Civil War began. She had escaped from slavery in Maryland in 1849, made her way north to freedom, and then — in an act of courage so extraordinary that it strains the capacity of language to describe it adequately — gone back. Repeatedly. Thirteen times, by the most commonly cited count, she returned to the South to guide other enslaved people to freedom through the Underground Railroad, moving through territory where her capture would have meant a return to slavery or death, relying on a network of contacts and a personal fearlessness that had led Frederick Douglass to write that he knew of no one who had done more for the liberation of enslaved people than Harriet Tubman.

When the Civil War began, Tubman brought those skills — the navigation of hostile territory, the management of intelligence networks, the assessment of risk and the exploitation of opportunity — to the Union war effort in South Carolina, where she was sent in 1862 under the auspices of the Union Army to serve as a nurse, a scout, and eventually the coordinator of a network of African American spies operating in Confederate-held territory.

The network she built drew on the same principles that had made the Underground Railroad effective: local knowledge, trusted contacts, the exploitation of the invisibility that the Confederate social order imposed on African Americans, and the motivation of people who had everything to gain from Union victory and everything to lose from Confederate survival. Her scouts — African American men who knew the local waterways, roads, and Confederate positions with the intimacy of people who had lived among them — provided Union commanders with intelligence that no white agent could have gathered with equivalent depth or reliability.

The culmination of Tubman's intelligence work in South Carolina came on the night of June 1 to 2, 1863 — the Combahee River Raid, conducted by Colonel James Montgomery with a force of African American Union soldiers from the 2nd South Carolina Infantry.

The raid's success depended entirely on intelligence. The Combahee River was mined — Confederate torpedoes had been placed in the water to destroy Union vessels attempting to navigate it. The locations of those mines were known to the enslaved people who had watched them being placed and who had provided that information to Tubman's network. Montgomery's gunboats navigated the Combahee in darkness, guided by pilots who knew exactly where the mines were because Tubman's intelligence had told them.

In a single night, the raid destroyed millions of dollars worth of Confederate rice plantations and supplies along the river banks — and freed 756 enslaved people, who came to the riverbanks in the darkness when word spread that the Union gunboats were coming. It was the largest single liberation of enslaved people by a military operation in the entire war, and it was made possible by an intelligence network run by a woman who had been born into slavery and who had spent her adult life doing things that were supposed to be impossible.

Tubman received no military pay for her intelligence work for much of the war — a fact that she spent decades attempting to have corrected, finally receiving a pension in 1899, more than thirty years after the war ended. She was awarded the Congressional Gold Medal posthumously in 2022, 103 years after her death.

The full history of African American intelligence contribution to the Union war effort will never be completely recovered, and honesty requires acknowledging that plainly.

The men and women who provided intelligence to Union forces operated in a world that kept no records of their activities — or kept records that named the white officers who received the intelligence while omitting the Black agents who gathered it. The debriefing reports that survive in Union military archives describe what was learned without always preserving the names of the people who taught it. The networks that Tubman and others built were designed for invisibility — and that invisibility, so essential to their operational effectiveness, also ensured their historical obscurity.

What the fragmentary record makes clear is this: that the Union possessed, in the enslaved and free Black population of the Confederate South, an intelligence advantage of incalculable value. That advantage was partially exploited and largely squandered by a Union military establishment that could not fully see past its own assumptions about the people whose knowledge it needed. And that the men and women who provided that intelligence — at personal risk that their white counterparts rarely faced in equivalent degree — did so out of a commitment to their own freedom and the freedom of their people that needed no external motivation and received, in most cases, no external recognition.

They were the most effective intelligence network of the Civil War. History is only beginning to give them their due.

The Cipher and the Key

Cryptography and Code-Breaking in the Civil War

T he message arrived in Richmond looking like nonsense.

That was the point. Strung together in groups of letters that meant nothing to the uninitiated — NQFDS LKRTZ MWPOA, or something equally impenetrable — it had traveled by courier from the western theater, encoded before it left and intended to remain unreadable to anyone who intercepted it along the way. The Confederate officer who received it reached for his brass cipher disk, aligned the rings to the agreed key word, and began working through the substitutions one letter at a time.

This was how the secret war communicated with itself. Not in the dramatic whispered exchanges of the spy novel but in the patient, painstaking work of encryption and decryption — letters becoming numbers becoming letters again, meaning hidden inside apparent gibberish, the whole elaborate machinery of coded communication running alongside the war's visible machinery of cannon and cavalry and infantry charge.

Both sides had secrets worth keeping. Both sides built systems to keep them. And both sides spent considerable energy trying to crack the other's systems before the other could crack theirs.

It was, in many respects, the most modern thing about an otherwise nineteenth century war.

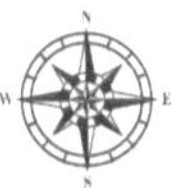

Before the Civil War, the United States Army had no cryptographic system worth the name.

Military commanders sent messages in plain language, relying on physical security — trusted couriers, sealed dispatches, the hope that interception would be unlikely — rather than encryption. It was a system that worked tolerably well in the age of horse and rider. It worked considerably less well in the age of the telegraph.

The telegraph had transformed military communication in ways that were still being understood when the war began. A message that would have taken days to travel by courier could now travel hundreds of miles in minutes — but it had to travel along wires that were physically vulnerable to interception, tapping, and capture. A wire could be cut. It could be tapped. The message moving along it, if sent in plain language, could be read by anyone with access to the line.

Both sides understood this problem from the war's earliest days. Neither side was fully prepared to solve it.

The Union's solution emerged from an unlikely source — the commercial telegraph industry, which had been wrestling with the security of its communications for years before the war began. Anson Stager was the general superintendent of the Western Union Telegraph Company when the war started, a compact and methodical Ohio man whose understanding of telegraph technology was matched by a practical intelligence about its vulnerabilities. He had been thinking about the problem of secure telegraph communication before anyone in Washington had thought to ask him about it.

His solution was the route cipher — an encryption system of elegant simplicity that proved, in practice, remarkably difficult to break.

The method worked like this. The message to be encrypted was written out in a grid — a rectangle of words, arranged in columns of a predetermined number. The columns were then read not in the obvious order but in a specific route — perhaps starting at the bottom of the third column, moving to the top of the first, then down the fifth, then up the second — a route known only to the sender and the authorized recipients. The resulting string of words looked like random gibberish to anyone who didn't know the route. To someone who did, it resolved instantly into the original message.

What made the system particularly effective was its variability. The route could be changed. The number of columns could be changed. Dummy words could be inserted to confuse anyone attempting to reconstruct the grid by frequency analysis. A cryptanalyst attempting to break a route cipher message without knowing the key variables faced a combinatorial problem of considerable difficulty — the number of possible routes through even a modest grid ran into the thousands.

Stager brought his system to the War Department in the summer of 1861, and it was adopted almost immediately as the standard encryption method for Union military telegraph communications. It was not perfect — no cipher system is — but it was substantially more secure than plain language transmission, and it was simple enough that telegraph operators could encrypt and decrypt messages quickly under operational conditions.

The man responsible for training those operators and managing the Union's telegraph cipher system was Major Thomas Eckert — but the daily work of the cipher office fell to a small group of young operators whose names have largely disappeared from the historical record. Among them was Charles Tinker.

Charles Tinker was twenty-two years old when the war began, a telegraph operator from Illinois who had been working the wires since his mid-teens and who possessed the particular combination of technical facility and mental agility that cipher work demanded. He was assigned to the War Department telegraph office in Washington — a cramped, cluttered room on the second floor of the War Department building, connected by wire to Union commands across the eastern theater and serving as the nerve center of Union military communications.

It was also, for much of the war, Abraham Lincoln's favorite room in Washington.

Lincoln came to the telegraph office almost daily — sometimes multiple times a day — drawn by what the telegraph operators who worked there later described as an almost physical need to know what was happening at the front. He would settle into a chair, ask for the message file, and read through the accumulated dispatches with the focused attention of a man for whom the contents of those messages represented something more than military intelligence. Each message from the front was a dispatch from the world that was consuming his presidency, and Lincoln read them with the same mix of hunger and dread that characterized his entire relationship with the war.

Tinker and his colleagues became, by proximity, among the people Lincoln spent the most time with during the war years. The operators later wrote about those hours with a mixture of professional pride and genuine affection — Lincoln asking questions, making occasional jokes, sometimes drafting responses in the telegraph office rather than returning to the White House, sitting in the corner with his long legs folded awkwardly under the table while the wires clicked around him.

What Lincoln was reading, in part, were intercepted Confederate messages.

The Union telegraph monitoring operation — tapping Confederate lines, capturing Confederate dispatch riders, seizing Confederate telegraph offices as Union forces advanced — produced a steady stream of encrypted Confederate communications that landed on the desks of Tinker and his colleagues for analysis. Breaking them required understanding the Confederate cipher system, which was a different animal from the Union's route cipher.

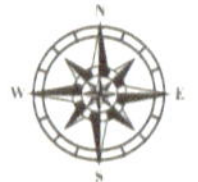

The Confederacy's primary cipher system was based on the Vigenère cipher — a polyalphabetic substitution cipher that had been considered unbreakable for so long that it was known in cryptographic circles as *le chiffre indéchiffrable.* The unbreakable cipher.

It wasn't.

The Vigenère cipher worked by using a keyword to shift each letter of the plaintext by a different amount — if the keyword was MANCHESTER, the first letter of the message was shifted by the value of M, the second by A, the third by N, and so on, cycling through the keyword repeatedly. The result was a ciphertext in which the same plaintext letter could be represented by different ciphertext letters depending on its position — defeating the simple frequency analysis that broke basic substitution ciphers.

The Confederate implementation used brass cipher disks — two concentric rings of letters that could be rotated relative to each other to perform the encryption and decryption. The disks were beautiful objects, precisely machined, small enough to fit in a coat pocket. Officers carried them the way they carried sidearms — as essential equipment for the work they were doing.

The Confederate cipher had two weaknesses that its architects either didn't recognize or didn't adequately address.

The first was the keywords. The Confederacy used only three keywords throughout the entire war — and those keywords, once discovered, unlocked every message encrypted with them. The Union cryptanalysts eventually identified all three. After that, intercepted Confederate messages were not puzzles to be solved. They were documents to be read.

The second weakness was operational — the same weakness that afflicts every security system that depends on physical objects. The cipher disk could be lost. Captured. Left behind in a retreat. And when it was gone, the people who needed to use it couldn't.

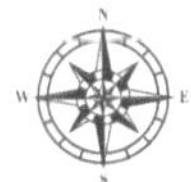

The fall of Vicksburg on July 4, 1863, was one of the turning points of the war — the moment the Confederacy lost control of the Mississippi River and with it the ability to move men and supplies between its eastern and western halves. It was also the occasion of one of the most revealing cryptographic episodes of the entire conflict.

Among the Confederate materials captured when Vicksburg fell was a cache of documents that included an encrypted message — a dispatch from Confederate President Jefferson Davis to General John Pemberton, the commander of the Vicksburg garrison, that had arrived too late to affect the outcome of the siege. The message had been encrypted using the Confederate cipher system. The cipher disk needed to decrypt it had been lost sometime during the siege — captured, destroyed, or simply misplaced in the chaos of a city under bombardment for forty-seven days.

Pemberton's officers had been unable to read the message from their own president.

Union cryptanalysts had no such difficulty. Working from their knowledge of the Confederate keyword system, they decrypted Davis's message and read it — a communication from the Confederate head of state to his besieged commander, arriving after the surrender that rendered it moot, now sitting in Union hands and telling its captors exactly what Jefferson Davis had been thinking about the defense of Vicksburg and the broader Confederate strategic situation in the west.

The specific contents of the message have been partially documented in postwar accounts, though the complete text has not been definitively established in the open historical record. What is documented is the basic fact of its capture and decryption — and what it illustrated about the fundamental asymmetry that had developed in the cipher war by mid-1863. The Union was reading Confederate messages. The Confederacy, in at least this instance, could not read its own.

The race between encryption and decryption that ran alongside the Civil War's visible battles was never fully won by either side — but the Union held the advantage for most of the conflict, for reasons that went beyond the specific vulnerabilities of the Confederate cipher system.

The Union's telegraph network was larger, better organized, and more systematically secured than the Confederacy's. The War Department telegraph office — where Tinker and his colleagues worked, where Lincoln read dispatches in the corner chair — was the hub of a communications system that connected Union commands across multiple theaters with a reliability and speed that the Confederacy's more improvised arrangements could not match. The Union invested in cipher security and in the training of cipher operators in ways the Confederacy did not consistently match.

None of this made Union communications perfectly secure. Confederate operators tapped Union lines. Confederate cavalry raids cut Union telegraph wires with frustrating regularity. Confederate agents in Washington — Rose Greenhow's network among them — gathered intelligence through human sources that no cipher system could protect against. The cipher war, like the intelligence war of which it was a part, was not a contest with clean victories and clear losers. It was a continuous, grinding competition in which advantage shifted and errors compounded and the difference between a message read and a message missed could be measured in the lives of men who never knew their fates had been decided by a brass disk and a keyword.

Charles Tinker survived the war. He continued working as a telegraph operator and later in the railroad industry, one of the thousands of young men whose specific contributions to the Union war effort were swallowed by the institutional anonymity of the organizations they served. He left behind some recollections of the telegraph office years — including his memories of Lincoln's visits, which constitute some of the more intimate portraits of the wartime president in the historical record.

Lincoln's favorite chair in the telegraph office, Tinker recalled, was positioned so that the president could see both the door and the window — old habits of situational awareness from a frontier lawyer's life, or perhaps something acquired in the years of living with the knowledge that people wanted him dead.

He sat in it for hours, reading the war one message at a time, in a room full of young men turning enemy secrets into plain language.

The cipher and the key. The message and the man who could read it.

That was the secret war's most essential transaction — repeated thousands of times across four years of conflict, in cramped offices and field tents and the back rooms of telegraph stations from Washington to Vicksburg, by people whose names the history books mostly forgot to record.

The Signal Corps

Rooftop Watchers and the Wig-Wag Revolution

Albert James Myer had a problem that had nothing to do with medicine.

He was an army surgeon by training — a Buffalo, New York doctor who had taken a commission in the Medical Corps and spent his early military career posted to the Texas frontier, where the distances were vast and the communication between scattered outposts was slow, unreliable, and occasionally fatal in its inadequacy. A message that took two days to travel by horse across the Texas desert was a message that arrived too late, and Myer had watched enough of those messages arrive to develop a consuming interest in the question of how military communication could be made faster.

The answer he arrived at was elegant, counterintuitive, and would change the nature of warfare.

Not a better horse. Not a faster rider. A flag.

One flag. Moved in specific patterns that encoded letters, which encoded words, which encoded messages that could travel at the speed of sight across distances that would have taken a courier hours to cover. The system Myer developed in the late 1850s — which he called wig-wag, for the waving motion of the flag — was based on a binary code of his own invention, derived in part from his knowledge of sign language for the deaf. Two basic movements — a wave to the left, a wave to the right — combined in sequences of varying length to represent every letter of the alphabet. A trained operator with a telescope could read a wig-wag message from fifteen miles away. In clear conditions, with a torch substituted for the flag, it worked at night.

He brought his invention to the Army in 1856. The Army took four years to pay attention.

The Signal Corps that Myer eventually built was the first dedicated military communications organization in American history — and it was born, like most military innovations, out of the specific failure that made its absence impossible to ignore any longer.

That failure was the First Battle of Bull Run.

But before Bull Run, before the war, before any of what followed, there was the training — and in that training lay one of the more remarkable ironies in the entire history of American military communication.

In the spring of 1861, with the war just beginning and the Army scrambling to build the organizational infrastructure that four years of conflict would require, Myer began training the first class of signal officers. The curriculum he developed covered the wig-wag code itself, the use of telescopes for reading distant signals, the selection and preparation of signal stations, and the operational procedures for integrating signal communication into battlefield command.

One of his students was a young West Point graduate named Edward Porter Alexander.

Alexander was twenty-six years old, brilliant, technically minded, and about to resign his Union Army commission to join the Confederacy. He paid close attention in Myer's class. He took careful notes. He learned the wig-wag system with the thoroughness of a man who understood he was going to need it — and who understood, perhaps better than Myer did at that moment, exactly how he was going to use it.

Within months, Alexander would turn everything Myer had taught him against the army that had trained him.

The First Battle of Bull Run on July 21, 1861, was supposed to be the battle that ended the war.

That, at least, was what Washington believed — what the crowds of civilians who had driven out from the capital with picnic baskets to watch believed, what the newspaper editors who had been running "On to Richmond" headlines believed, what the Union Army commanders who had been pressured by public opinion and presidential anxiety into moving before they were ready believed. One battle, one Confederate defeat, one short march to Richmond, and the rebellion would collapse under the weight of its own hubris.

What happened instead was a catastrophe — and at the center of that catastrophe, in a way that has never been fully acknowledged in the popular history of the battle, was a flag.

Edward Porter Alexander had been assigned to establish a Confederate signal station on a hill called Signal Hill, over-looking the Bull Run battlefield from the Confederate left flank. His position gave him a view of the Union movements that Confederate ground commanders, obscured by the terrain and the smoke of the early fighting, could not replicate. He was watching through his telescope when he saw something that changed the battle.

Union troops — a significant force — were moving along a road to the west of the main Confederate position. They were attempting to flank the Confederate left, to swing around and strike from a direction the Confederate line was not prepared to defend. If the movement succeeded, the Confederate position would be compromised before the reinforcements that General Joseph Johnston was rushing from the Shenandoah Valley could arrive to stabilize it.

Alexander reached for his flags.

The message he sent — wig-wagged in the system his former instructor had taught him, readable by Confederate signal officers on the far end of the line — was one of the most consequential single communications of the entire war. Its text, as Alexander later recorded it, was direct: the enemy was turning the Confederate flank.

Confederate commanders received the warning and reacted. Troops were shifted. The flanking movement was met rather than allowed to develop unopposed. The battle that followed was brutal and confused — as Civil War battles invariably were — but the Confederate position held long enough for Johnston's reinforcements to arrive and tip the balance. The Union Army broke. The rout that followed sent soldiers and civilians fleeing together down the roads toward Washington in scenes that shocked a Northern public that had expected a quick and decisive victory.

Albert Myer, watching from the Union side of the battlefield, understood exactly what had happened. His system had been used against him by the man he had trained to use it.

The Signal Corps that emerged from Bull Run's lessons was a different organization from the tentative beginning Myer had been building before the battle. The war had demonstrated, with brutal clarity, the operational value of real-time battlefield communication — and both sides moved quickly to develop the capability that demonstration demanded.

The network of signal stations that the Union Signal Corps established across the Virginia theater over the following months was, by the standards of its time, a remarkable feat of military organization. Stations were established on rooftops in Washington, on the heights above the Potomac crossings, on hilltops across northern Virginia, and on specially constructed wooden towers that could be erected in days and dismantled just as quickly when the army moved. Each station was manned by trained signal officers who maintained constant watch through their telescopes, reading incoming messages and transmitting outgoing ones in a relay system that could move intelligence from the front lines to army headquarters in minutes.

The observation function was as important as the communication function — sometimes more so. A signal officer stationed on a commanding height with a good telescope was, in effect, an intelligence collection platform — able to observe enemy movements, count troops and artillery, identify unit flags and formations, and transmit that information in real time to commanders who needed it. The rooftop watchers of Washington could see across the Potomac into Confederate Virginia. The signal towers on the heights above the Rappahannock could read the dispositions of Confederate forces on the opposite bank. The observation network that Myer built was, in modern terms, a persistent surveillance capability — imperfect, weather-dependent, and limited by line of sight, but far superior to anything that had existed in American military practice before.

The Confederacy built a parallel system under Alexander's direction — signal stations on the heights of northern Virginia that watched the Union signal stations watching them, each side reading the other's flag movements through their telescopes, each side changing its codes when it suspected the other had broken them, in a continuous cat-and-mouse game of interception and counter-interception that ran alongside every major operation in the eastern theater.

The interception of enemy flag messages was not, it turned out, particularly difficult — at least not in the early part of the war.

Both sides were using variants of the same basic wig-wag code that Myer had developed, and a signal officer who knew the system could read an enemy transmission as easily as a friendly one, provided he had a line of sight to the sending station and knew the current code key. The code keys — the specific letter assignments that translated flag movements into text — were changed periodically to prevent this, but the changes were not always made promptly, and the discipline required to ensure that old keys were completely retired before new ones were introduced was not always maintained under operational conditions.

There are documented accounts, from both Union and Confederate signal officers, of reading enemy messages in real time during battles — watching the flags on the opposite ridge and decoding the transmission as it was being sent, sometimes faster than the intended recipient could decode it. The operational implications of this were significant. A commander who knew what the enemy's signal officer was telling his general had information of immediate tactical value — information about intentions, about troop movements, about the coordination of attacks that were being planned for the next hour.

The response to systematic interception was the development of more complex code systems — moving beyond the basic wig-wag alphabet to layered encryption that required additional keys to decode. But complexity introduced its own problems. A code system complex enough to defeat interception was also complex enough to slow transmission significantly — and speed was the fundamental operational advantage that signal communication existed to provide. The tension between security and speed was never fully resolved during the war, and both sides paid for their compromises in messages read by the wrong eyes.

Albert Myer spent much of the war fighting a battle that had nothing to do with the Confederacy.

The Signal Corps he had created was, from its earliest days, contested organizational territory — claimed by the telegraph operators of the Military Telegraph Service, who argued that wire communication made flag signaling obsolete, and by the regular army bureaucracy, which viewed Myer's independent-minded operation with the institutional suspicion that the established always reserve for the innovative. Myer was eventually removed from command of the Signal Corps in November 1863 — relieved by Secretary of War Edwin Stanton in a dispute over the relationship between the

Signal Corps and the Military Telegraph that had more to do with bureaucratic politics than operational effectiveness.

He spent the final years of the war in bureaucratic exile, watching the organization he had built continue to operate under other commanders, contributing to operations he was no longer directing. He was reinstated after the war and eventually promoted to brigadier general — the first Chief Signal Officer of the United States Army, a title that acknowledged belatedly what his invention had contributed.

He also founded, in 1870, the organization that would become the National Weather Service — applying the same principle of distributed observation stations communicating in real time that he had developed for military signaling to the problem of weather prediction across a continent. The rooftop watchers had a longer legacy than anyone at Bull Run could have anticipated.

Edward Porter Alexander became one of the Confederacy's most capable artillery commanders — the officer who coordinated the massive artillery bombardment that preceded Pickett's Charge at Gettysburg, who recognized before the charge began that it was unlikely to succeed and said so, and who wrote after the war one of the most honest and analytically rigorous Confederate memoirs of the entire conflict. He lived until 1910, long enough to see the communication revolution his former instructor had set in motion transformed by technologies that made the wig-wag flag look as primitive as the horse messenger had looked in 1861.

He never, in any of his writing, expressed regret about using Myer's system against Myer's army.

He was a soldier. It was a war. The flag said what it needed to say, and the battle went the way it went.

That was enough.

The Spy in the Attic

Elizabeth Van Lew and the Richmond Underground

The neighbors had a name for her.

Crazy Bet. Said with a shake of the head, a knowing look, the particular mixture of pity and contempt that Richmond society reserved for one of its own who had gone wrong somewhere and couldn't find her way back. She walked too fast. She talked to herself. She dressed oddly and kept odd hours and had opinions about things that women of her station were not supposed to have opinions about — strong opinions, expressed without apology, in a city where the social contract required a certain performance of genteel agreement from women of the better families.

Elizabeth Van Lew performed no such thing.

She had grown up in one of Richmond's finest houses — the Van Lew mansion on Church Hill, overlooking the city from one of its commanding heights, the kind of address that announced family and money and the particular confidence that came with generations of both. Her father had been a successful hardware merchant. Her mother was from Philadelphia. Elizabeth herself had been sent north for her education, to a Quaker school in Philadelphia where the arguments against slavery were not abstract philosophy but lived conviction, and where a young woman from a Virginia slaveholding family encountered ideas that she could not afterwards unfind.

She came home to Richmond with those ideas intact. She freed the people her family had enslaved. And she waited, with the patience of someone who understood that the reckoning she believed was coming would arrive eventually, for the war that would make her useful.

It came in April 1861. Virginia seceded. The Confederacy established its capital in Richmond. And Elizabeth Van Lew, forty-three years old, wealthy, socially prominent, and burning with a conviction that her city and her state had chosen catastrophically wrong, began to build.

The eccentricity was at least partly a performance.

Not entirely — Van Lew was genuinely unconventional by the standards of Richmond society, and the convictions that made her unconventional were genuine. But the Crazy Bet persona that she cultivated with such apparent artlessness served a specific operational purpose: it made her unthreatening. A woman who talked to herself and walked too fast and held peculiar views about the moral status of enslaved people was a social embarrassment, possibly a figure of pity, certainly not someone to be taken seriously as a security threat.

Confederate Richmond did not take her seriously as a security threat for most of the war. That was precisely what she needed.

Her early resistance activities were relatively overt — visiting Union prisoners held at Libby Prison, bringing them food and books and medicines, passing messages in and out of the prison through the social cover that her status as a charitable Richmond lady provided. Confederate authorities were aware of her prison visits and uncomfortable with them, but prosecuting a woman of her social standing for charitable work was politically awkward, and the intelligence value of what she was doing was not immediately apparent to the people watching her.

It was immediately apparent to Van Lew.

The Union officers held at Libby Prison were a source of intelligence flowing in both directions. They told her what they knew about Confederate military dispositions and movements — information gathered before their capture that she transmitted to Union contacts. She told them what she had observed in Richmond — troop movements, supply shipments, the conversations she had overheard at social gatherings where people spoke freely in front of Crazy Bet because Crazy Bet didn't really count. And she helped them escape when she could — hiding officers in a secret room in the Van Lew mansion, a concealed space above the main house that she had prepared for exactly this purpose, moving them through a network of safe houses toward Union lines when the opportunity presented itself.

The attic room was real. Union officers who used it described it in postwar accounts — a hidden space, accessible through a concealed entrance, furnished simply, lit by a small window that overlooked the city below. It was the physical heart of Van Lew's operation in Richmond, the place where the secret war conducted itself in the most literal possible sense, inside the walls of one of the city's most prominent houses while Confederate society went about its business on the streets below.

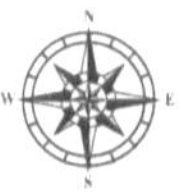

The network Van Lew built over the course of the war was more sophisticated than the improvised charitable operation it appeared to be from the outside.

She developed a cipher for her communications — a system for encoding messages that she transmitted to Union intelligence through a relay of trusted contacts between Richmond and the Union lines. She used a book cipher, in which specific words in a pre-agreed text were referenced by page, line, and word number — a system that produced encoded messages which looked, to anyone who intercepted them, like random strings of numbers. She hid messages in the hollowed-out soles of shoes, in the false bottoms of food containers, in the bindings of books sent to prisoners at Libby. Her farm outside the city served as a relay station — messages passed through it on their way north, carried by people whose ordinary movements between the farm and the city provided natural cover.

She recruited agents — Black and white, free and enslaved, men and women — with the careful assessment of someone who understood that a single wrong choice could destroy everything. The network that resulted was small enough to be manageable and large enough to be effective, compartmentalized so that the exposure of one agent could not unravel the whole.

General Ulysses Grant, when he took command of Union forces in 1864 and established his headquarters at City Point outside Richmond, began receiving intelligence from inside the Confederate capital that was more detailed and more reliable than anything his predecessors had been getting. He later wrote that the intelligence from Richmond during the final year of the war was of great value — and that its source was the Van Lew network. He communicated with Van Lew directly, sending her requests for specific intelligence and receiving her reports through the relay system she had developed.

The woman Confederate Richmond had dismissed as Crazy Bet was providing the commander of all Union armies with intelligence from inside the enemy capital.

The most remarkable claim associated with Van Lew's network — and the one that requires the most careful historical handling — involves a woman named Mary Elizabeth Bowser.

Bowser had been born into slavery in the Van Lew household. Van Lew had freed her, educated her, and at some point during the war — the precise timing and circumstances are not fully established in the documentary record — placed her as a servant in the household of Confederate President Jefferson Davis at the Confederate White House in Richmond.

What Bowser did there, according to accounts that have circulated since the war, was extraordinary. She was, by multiple accounts, possessed of a photographic memory — able to read a document once and reproduce its contents accurately from memory. Working as a servant in Davis's household, she had access to rooms where Confederate documents were handled, meetings where Confederate strategy was discussed, conversations that the men conducting them considered private because the Black woman serving their meals was, in the logic of the Confederate social order, not really there.

She was there. She was reading. She was remembering. And she was passing what she learned to Van Lew's network.

The intelligence that flowed from the Confederate White House — if the accounts are accurate — would have been among the most valuable of the entire war. Cabinet discussions. Strategic plans. The private communications of the Confederate president. Intelligence of this quality, reliably sourced from the heart of Confederate government, would represent an espionage achievement of the first order by any standard.

The historical record, however, requires caution here — and Van Lew's own commitment to protecting her agents means that caution is genuinely warranted rather than merely reflexive.

Bowser's name does not appear in Van Lew's wartime journals — which Van Lew kept in cipher and which she partially destroyed after the war, apparently to protect the identities of people who might still face retaliation. The specific intelligence products that can be definitively attributed to Bowser's observations at the Confederate White House have not been identified in Union military records. The most detailed accounts of her activities rely on sources compiled decades after the war, when the documentary trail had grown cold and the incentives for embellishment had grown warm.

What is documented is this: Van Lew did place African American agents in positions that gave them access to Confederate information. She did have a connection to Mary Bowser. And the intelligence she provided to Grant's headquarters in 1864 and 1865 was detailed enough and reliable enough that its sourcing clearly reached into Confederate government circles.

Whether Bowser was reading Jefferson Davis's papers at his dining room table is a claim that the available evidence supports as plausible without establishing as proven. It is presented here as the most credible account of what may have happened — not as established fact.

What can be said without qualification is that whatever Van Lew's network was doing inside the Confederate White House, it was working.

Richmond knew, by the end of the war, what Elizabeth Van Lew had done.

The city had suspected for some time — the visits to Libby Prison, the oddly specific quality of her eccentricity, the fact that a woman of her intelligence and means had never quite fit the role that Confederate Richmond had assigned her. When Union forces entered Richmond in April 1865 and Van Lew raised a large American flag over the Van Lew mansion — a flag she had kept hidden throughout the war, waiting for this moment — the question of whose side she had been on was definitively answered for anyone who had still been wondering.

Richmond did not forgive her.

The ostracism that followed was systematic and complete. Former neighbors crossed the street to avoid her. Former friends declined to receive her. Shopkeepers who had done business with the Van Lew family for generations found reasons to be unavailable. The social world that she had moved through for four decades — the world she had used as cover and as a resource for her intelligence operation — closed against her with the cold efficiency of a community that had decided she was a traitor to everything it valued.

She had been, of course. Deliberately, committedly, and without apology.

President Ulysses Grant appointed her postmaster of Richmond in 1869 — a recognition of her wartime service that was also, in the context of Reconstruction-era Richmond, a provocation. She held the position for eight years, conducting the work with the same thoroughness she had brought to everything else, and enduring the social hostility of the city she administered with the equanimity of someone who had spent four years operating a spy network under the noses of Confederate intelligence and found that considerably more demanding.

She spent the last decades of her life in the Van Lew mansion, her fortune largely gone — consumed by the wartime expenses of running a spy network and by the costs of a post-war existence in which her social isolation made the ordinary transactions of community life difficult and expensive. She died in 1900, at seventy-two, in the house where the secret room had hidden Union officers and the cipher had encoded dispatches for Grant's headquarters.

The friends who remembered her at the end were few. The acknowledgment from the government whose cause she had served was minimal. The mainstream history of the Civil War, for most of the century that followed, managed to tell its story without her name appearing more than occasionally in footnotes.

She deserved considerably better than footnotes.

The intelligence network she built in Richmond — improvised, carefully concealed, professionally maintained, connected to the highest levels of Union military command — was among the most effective espionage operations of the entire war. She ran it from a house on Church Hill in a city that thought she was crazy, under the noses of Confederate authorities who never fully grasped what was happening inside one of their most prominent addresses, at personal and financial cost that she bore without ever complaining and apparently without regret.

Crazy Bet. The name they gave her said everything about what they saw and nothing about what was actually there.

What was actually there was one of the finest intelligence officers the Civil War had ever produced.

The Balloon Corps

Thaddeus Lowe and Aerial Intelligence

T he telegram read: *"This point of vantage ought not to be lost to the country."*

It was June 18, 1861. The man who sent it was floating five hundred feet above the White House lawn in a hydrogen balloon called the Enterprise, looking down at a city that was simultaneously the capital of a nation and the nervous center of a war that had just begun. The man who received it was Abraham Lincoln, standing somewhere below in a world that had never before received a telegram from the sky.

Thaddeus Sobieski Constantine Lowe — the name alone was an event — was thirty years old, self-educated, and possessed of the particular combination of showmanship and genuine technical ability that the nineteenth century occasionally produced in men who had grown up outside the institutions that usually sorted such things out. He had been fascinated by balloons since his teens, had built his first one at twenty-three, and had spent the years since making ascents across the eastern United States with the slightly reckless confidence of someone who had decided that the air was not actually dangerous if you paid attention.

He had come to Washington with an idea and a balloon. Lincoln, who was constitutionally inclined toward practical innovation and who had been looking at this war with the eyes of a man trying to understand something that kept moving faster than his information about it, came outside to look up.

What happened next would create the world's first military aerial reconnaissance unit — and end, three years later, in a bureaucratic squabble so petty and so consequential that men died for it.

Before Lowe, the highest a military commander could see was the top of a hill.

That sounds obvious. It was also a profound operational limitation that most commanders had simply accepted as a feature of the landscape — like mud or weather or the fact that the enemy didn't publish its plans in advance. You put scouts on the high ground. You sent cavalry forward to feel out the enemy's position. You waited for prisoners who might tell you something useful. And then you committed your army to a course of action based on information that was hours old before it reached you, filtered through the observations of men on horseback who could see perhaps two miles on a clear day.

Lowe, floating above the Potomac in the summer of 1861, could see twenty.

The demonstration he gave Lincoln was convincing enough that the president directed him to work with the Army — which was not, it turned out, quite the same thing as the Army directing itself to work with him. The military bureaucracy of 1861 had the institutional relationship with innovation that military bureaucracies usually have, which is to say a cautious and occasionally hostile one, and Lowe spent weeks navigating a procurement system that had not been designed with civilian aeronauts in mind before he received authorization to build his balloon fleet.

He built seven balloons. He recruited a team of aeronauts — most of them from the civilian ballooning world he had inhabited before the war, men who understood hydrogen and silk and the particular physics of staying aloft while someone below was shooting at you. He worked out the logistics of producing hydrogen in the field — a process that required mobile generators, sulfuric acid, and iron filings, and that could fill a balloon in a matter of hours rather than the days that earlier methods required. And he solved, with characteristic ingenuity, the problem of communicating what he saw.

The telegraph wire ran up the tether rope.

It sounds simple because it was — a physical wire connecting the balloon's basket to a telegraph set on the ground, allowing real-time transmission of observations from altitude to commanders who needed them. Lowe had been the first person to send a telegram from an aircraft. He would build an entire intelligence system around the principle.

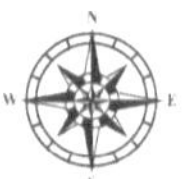

The Peninsula Campaign of the spring and summer of 1862 was the Balloon Corps' finest hour — and the clearest demonstration of what aerial intelligence could contribute to military operations when commanders were willing to use it.

McClellan's army was moving up the Virginia Peninsula toward Richmond, and Lowe's balloons were moving with it

— a fleet of hydrogen-filled observation platforms that rose above the tree lines and river bottoms and gave Union commanders a view of Confederate positions that no cavalry scout could replicate. The balloons were tethered, controlled, repositioned as the army moved. Lowe himself made hundreds of ascents during the campaign, spending hours aloft with sketch pad and telescope, building a picture of Confederate dispositions that accumulated detail the way a photograph accumulates light — slowly, precisely, one observation at a time.

The observation of the Confederate evacuation of Yorktown in May 1862 is among the Balloon Corps' best-documented intelligence contributions. The Confederate garrison at Yorktown, under General John Magruder, had been conducting one of the more impressive theatrical performances of the war — using a small force to simulate the presence of a much larger one, marching troops in circles through gaps in the fortifications where Union observers on the ground could see them, creating the impression of a heavily defended position that was actually held by far fewer men than McClellan believed.

Lowe went up.

From altitude the theater was considerably less convincing. Confederate troops marching in circles to simulate larger numbers look, from five hundred feet, like Confederate troops marching in circles. The fortifications that had seemed formidable from ground level revealed themselves, when viewed from above, as partially constructed earthworks with gaps and weaknesses that the ground perspective had concealed. More importantly, when the Confederates eventually decided to abandon Yorktown and fall back toward Richmond, Lowe's observers spotted the evacuation before Union ground commanders — who were waiting for cavalry reports that were slower and less complete — had confirmed it.

The intelligence arrived in time to allow McClellan to pursue. Whether McClellan pursued with the aggressiveness the intelligence warranted is a separate question — one whose answer illuminates McClellan rather than Lowe.

The Battle of Fair Oaks at the end of May 1862 gave the Balloon Corps its most dramatic operational moment — and produced one of the more remarkable scenes of the entire war.

Lowe was aloft on May 31 when the battle began below him — a confused, costly engagement in swampy ground south of the Chickahominy River, triggered when Confederate General Joseph Johnston launched an attack on a Union corps that had been isolated on the wrong side of the river by flooding. From his basket, Lowe could see things that no one on the ground could see — the Confederate attack formations, the Union positions under pressure, the movement of reinforcements on both sides, the shape of a battle that was, from ground level, an incomprehensible noise of musketry and artillery in thick woods.

He sent telegrams.

The wire ran down the tether rope to the ground station, and the ground station relayed to headquarters, and headquarters attempted to translate the aerial perspective into orders that made sense to men who could not see what Lowe could see. The translation was imperfect — the gap between the observer's bird's-eye view and the commander's ground-level reality was not always bridgeable by telegraph — but the intelligence Lowe provided about Confederate movements contributed to the Union's ability to stabilize a battle that had begun badly.

He was doing this, it bears noting, while people on the ground were shooting at him.

Confederate infantry fired at Union observation balloons whenever they presented a target — rifles, artillery, whatever was available. The balloons were difficult targets at altitude, and hydrogen, despite its flammability, proved less catastrophically vulnerable to rifle fire than one might have expected — a small hole in a balloon envelope leaked gas slowly enough that the balloon could usually be winched down before it became critical. But the psychological experience of floating above an active battlefield while musket balls passed through the fabric of your aircraft was not one that many men would have chosen voluntarily.

Lowe chose it hundreds of times.

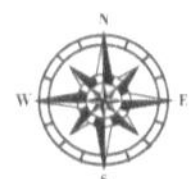

The Confederates, to their credit, adapted.

The response to Union aerial observation was not limited to shooting at balloons — though they did that too, with limited success. Confederate engineers began constructing camouflage screens around artillery positions and fortifications in areas they knew were visible to Union observers. Dummy artillery positions — logs shaped and painted to resemble cannon, positioned to draw observer attention away from actual gun emplacements — appeared along the Confederate lines. Troops were moved at night when possible, under cover that limited aerial observation. Supply routes were chosen partly for the tree cover they offered against the eye in the sky.

The Confederacy also built its own balloon.

Or rather — and this detail is one of the more charming footnotes in the entire war — they improvised one. Unable to obtain the silk and hydrogen equipment that Lowe's operation required, Confederate engineers in Richmond collected silk dress fabric — contributed, by some accounts, by patriotic Richmond ladies, though the precise provenance of the material varies across different tellings — and sewed it into a balloon envelope that was inflated with illuminating gas from the Richmond gas mains. The resulting craft, known variously as the Silk Dress Balloon or the Gas Bag, made a handful of ascents over the Richmond area before being captured when the vessel carrying it on the James River ran aground and was seized by Union forces.

It was the Confederacy's entire balloon program, beginning and end.

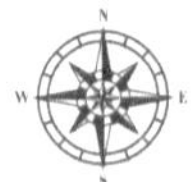

The Union Balloon Corps died not from Confederate action but from paperwork.

The bureaucratic situation that destroyed it had been building since the Corps' creation — a structural tension between Lowe's status as a civilian contractor and the military chain of command he was supposed to support. Lowe reported to the Corps of Engineers, which resented his independence. He had enemies in the quartermaster's office who questioned his expenses. The telegraph operators he needed were controlled by a different command than the balloons they were supposed to support. Nobody agreed on who paid for the hydrogen.

It was, in short, the kind of organizational dysfunction that military bureaucracies generate when they encounter innovations that don't fit their existing categories — and it ground Lowe down with a patience and thoroughness that Confederate artillery had failed to achieve.

In April 1863, the Army cut Lowe's pay — a reduction so significant that it amounted to a declaration that his services were not valued. Lowe resigned. His chief aeronaut, John Starkweather, attempted to keep the operation running but lacked Lowe's technical expertise and organizational drive. By August 1863 the Balloon Corps had effectively ceased to exist.

The military intelligence vacuum its absence created was real and documented. Union commanders in the Virginia theater lost the aerial observation capability they had been using for two years, at precisely the moment when Grant's operations against Richmond were entering their most demanding phase. The hills and tree lines that Lowe's balloons had seen over were opaque again. The Confederate positions that had been visible from five hundred feet were invisible again from ground level.

The Army would not have a dedicated aerial reconnaissance capability again until the First World War — fifty years later, when the technology had changed beyond recognition but the operational principle Lowe had demonstrated above the White House lawn in June 1861 remained exactly what it had always been.

Get above it. Look down. Tell someone what you see.

Lowe went home to New Hampshire. He spent the postwar decades in various business ventures — gas production, a mountain railway in California, schemes of varying ambition and varying success. He applied for a pension based on his wartime service. The application was denied. The government that had used his balloons above the Peninsula and above Fair Oaks did not, in the end, consider his contribution worth a pension.

He died in 1913, at eighty years old, largely forgotten by the military establishment that had discarded him fifty years before.

The telegram from the sky. The wire down the tether rope. The view that nobody else had.

Gone, because the paperwork didn't work out.

CONFEDERATE

The Rose of Washington

Rose O'Neal Greenhow and the Confederate Spy Ring

W ashington in the spring of 1861 was a city of drawing rooms and secrets, and Rose O'Neal Greenhow moved through both with equal mastery.

She was forty-four years old when the war began — a widow of considerable social standing, dark-eyed and imperious, possessed of the kind of beauty that had not diminished with age so much as deepened into something more formidable. Her husband, Robert Greenhow, had been a physician and scholar of some distinction before his death in 1854, and the social connections they had built together in Washington's political world had survived him intact. Rose had cultivated those connections with the deliberate attention of a woman who understood that in Washington, who you knew was the only currency that mattered.

She knew everyone.

Among her intimates she counted John C. Calhoun — the South Carolina senator and theorist of states' rights whose political philosophy had shaped the ideology of secession — whose protégée she had been since her arrival in Washington as a young woman from Maryland. She counted James Buchanan, the outgoing president, who had valued her political judgment enough to consult her regularly during his administration. She counted senators, cabinet members, military officers, and foreign diplomats — the full constellation of Washington power — and she had used those relationships to build a social position so secure that even the most cautious man in the capital felt comfortable speaking freely in her parlor.

That was exactly what she had intended.

Rose O'Neal Greenhow's Confederate sympathies were not a secret in Washington — she had never bothered to conceal them, calculating correctly that a woman of her social standing could express Southern sympathies without attracting the suspicion that the same views would have generated in a man of military age. She had been born in Maryland, raised on the political philosophy of Calhoun, and had watched the election of Abraham Lincoln with a contempt she made no effort to disguise.

What was a secret — carefully, professionally kept — was the use to which she was putting those sympathies.

Her recruitment into Confederate intelligence came through Thomas Jordan — a former United States Army officer who had resigned his commission to join the Confederacy and who, before leaving Washington in the spring of 1861, approached Greenhow with a proposition and a cipher. The cipher was simple — a twenty-six symbol substitution code that Jordan had developed for communicating with Confederate intelligence — and Greenhow learned it quickly. Jordan gave her a contact in Confederate General P.G.T. Beauregard's headquarters and left her to build whatever network she could from her position at the center of Washington society.

What she built was extraordinary.

The network Greenhow constructed in the spring and summer of 1861 was not the elaborate organizational structure of a professional intelligence service. It was something more organic and in some ways more effective — a web of personal relationships, social connections, and carefully cultivated sources that extended from the parlors of Washington's political elite to the offices of the War Department itself. Her sources included military officers who visited her home, politicians who confided in her at social events, and at least one young woman — Betty Duvall, a Confederate sympathizer from a prominent Maryland family — who served as a courier, carrying Greenhow's encoded messages through Union lines to Confederate headquarters.

She was not, by the standards of professional intelligence work, a careful operator. She kept documents in her home. She conducted meetings that a more cautious handler would have avoided. She relied on the assumption — not unreasonable given the social realities of the time — that a respectable Washington widow would not be suspected of espionage. In the summer of 1861, that assumption was correct. The Union had no counterintelligence capability worth the name, and the idea that the most prominent drawing rooms in Washington were being used to gather intelligence for the Confederacy had not yet penetrated the consciousness of the men responsible for the capital's security.

They would learn.

The intelligence that Rose Greenhow transmitted before the First Battle of Bull Run on July 21, 1861, is among the most consequential acts of espionage in American military history — and among the most documented, which makes it possible to assess its impact with more precision than is usually available for Civil War intelligence operations.

In the days before the battle, Greenhow sent two messages to Confederate General P.G.T. Beauregard at Manassas. The first, carried by Betty Duvall, reported that the Union Army under General Irvin McDowell was preparing to advance and provided details about the planned route and timing of the movement. Duvall carried the message encoded and hidden in her hair — a detail that has the slightly theatrical quality of a spy novel but is documented in Beauregard's own postwar account. The second message, transmitted as the Union advance was beginning, provided additional detail about McDowell's order of battle and the specific direction of his planned flanking movement.

Beauregard's response to this intelligence was immediate and consequential. He sent urgent requests to Confederate General Joseph Johnston in the Shenandoah Valley to bring his forces to Manassas by rail — the first use of railroads to move troops to a battlefield in American history — and adjusted his defensive dispositions based on what Greenhow had told him about the direction of the Union advance.

[Historical note: The precise contribution of Greenhow's intelligence to the Confederate victory at Bull Run has been debated by historians. Beauregard himself, in his postwar memoir, credited her information as significant in his preparations. Some historians have argued that the Confederate victory resulted primarily from the fighting qualities of Confederate troops and the tactical failures of Union commanders rather than from intelligence advantages. The most balanced assessment is that Greenhow's intelligence contributed to Confederate preparedness without being solely decisive —

it was one significant factor among several in a Confederate victory that had multiple causes.]

The Union army was routed. The battle that Northern newspapers had been calling a quick and decisive end to the rebellion turned into a catastrophic retreat, with Union soldiers and Washington civilians who had come out to watch the battle fleeing together down the roads toward the capital in scenes of complete disorder. The Confederacy celebrated. Jefferson Davis, who had arrived at the battlefield in the final hours of the fighting, sent Greenhow a message of personal thanks.

She was, at that moment, the most effective intelligence agent in the Confederate service. She was also, though she did not yet know it, being watched.

Allan Pinkerton had been aware of Greenhow's sympathies since the spring of 1861, but awareness of sympathies and evidence of espionage were different things, and Pinkerton was too experienced an investigator to move before he had what he needed. He assigned operatives to surveil her home on Sixteenth Street — a task complicated by the social prominence that made unusual activity around the house immediately visible — and built his case through patient observation and the cultivation of sources within her circle.

By late July 1861, following Bull Run and the evidence that Confederate commanders had possessed detailed advance intelligence about Union movements, the urgency of the investigation increased significantly. On August 23, 1861, Pinkerton moved.

He arrived at Greenhow's home himself — accompanied by several operatives and, in an irony he later noted with some satisfaction, catching her in the act of meeting with a Union Army captain who was, apparently, one of her sources. The captain was arrested. Greenhow was placed under house arrest in her own home, which Pinkerton converted into an improvised detention facility, housing other suspected female Confederate sympathizers there as well.

The house arrest proved, almost immediately, to be an inadequate containment measure. Greenhow continued her intelligence activities from within her own home — communicating with Confederate agents through her servants, through visitors, through the window of her house that overlooked the street, using a variety of improvised methods that demonstrated both her resourcefulness and the fundamental difficulty of the Union's position. Arresting a prominent Washington socialite was politically awkward. Treating her with the severity that her actual intelligence activities warranted was more awkward still.

In January 1862 she was transferred to the Old Capitol Prison — a converted boarding house near the Capitol building that had been pressed into service as a detention facility for political prisoners and Confederate sympathizers. The transfer did not stop her.

Rose Greenhow's imprisonment in the Old Capitol Prison is one of the more remarkable episodes in the history of Civil War intelligence — remarkable not for the conditions of her confinement, which were relatively comfortable by the standards of the time, but for the degree to which she continued to operate as an intelligence agent from inside a Union prison.

She conducted herself throughout her imprisonment with the imperious confidence of a woman who considered herself a prisoner of war rather than a criminal, and who was determined to make her captors understand the distinction. She refused to sign loyalty oaths. She protested her conditions in letters to government officials. She gave interviews to sympathetic journalists that were published in newspapers on both sides of the conflict. And she continued, through methods that Union prison authorities were never entirely able to suppress, to pass information and communications to Confederate contacts outside the prison walls.

The Union's response to this situation was ultimately pragmatic. Keeping Rose Greenhow in prison was producing more propaganda value for the Confederacy than intelligence value for the Union. In the spring of 1862, she was offered an exchange — release and transport to Confederate territory in exchange for a commitment not to return to Union lines.

She accepted and crossed into Confederate Virginia in June 1862 — where she was received as a heroine. Jefferson Davis granted her an audience. Confederate officials feted her as a celebrity of the cause. She had done what few intelligence agents of any era have managed: she had been caught, imprisoned, and emerged from the experience with her reputation not merely intact but enhanced.

The Confederacy sent Rose Greenhow to Europe in August 1862 — an unofficial diplomatic mission that used her celebrity and her social gifts in service of the Confederate effort to secure recognition and support from the major European powers.

She was received with a warmth that reflected the genuine sympathy for the Confederate cause that existed in certain segments of European aristocratic society. She met Napoleon III of France and his Empress Eugénie. She was granted an audience with Queen Victoria. She moved through the drawing rooms of London and Paris with the same mastery she had demonstrated in Washington, charming the powerful and collecting the expressions of sympathy that were, ultimately, all that the Confederacy's European diplomacy ever produced. Britain and France never recognized the Confederate government. The sympathy of their ruling classes never translated into the official support that Confederate strategy required.

Greenhow wrote a memoir during her time in Europe — My Imprisonment and the First Year of Abolition Rule at Washington, published in London in 1863 — that presented her story from her own perspective with considerable rhetorical skill and selective historical memory. It was a Confederate propaganda document as much as a personal account, and it served that purpose effectively in the European market for which it was primarily intended.

By the summer of 1864 she was ready to return to the Confederacy. The war had turned decisively against the South — Gettysburg and Vicksburg had shattered Confederate strategic prospects — but Greenhow's commitment to the cause had not wavered. She boarded the blockade runner Condor at Falmouth, England, in August 1864, carrying Confederate dispatches and, according to accounts that have been generally accepted by historians, a significant amount of gold — payment for her European services or funds for Confederate use, depending on the account.

The Condor reached the North Carolina coast on the night of October 1, 1864, and ran aground on a sandbar near the mouth of the Cape Fear River while attempting to evade the USS Niphon, a Union blockade vessel that had spotted it in the darkness.

The Condor was stuck but not sinking — the captain believed it could be freed on the next tide and urged his passengers to remain aboard. Rose Greenhow refused. She was unwilling to be captured by Union forces — the prospect of a second imprisonment, and the dispatches she was carrying, made that outcome unacceptable. She demanded to be put ashore in a small boat.

The captain acquiesced. A rowboat was lowered. Greenhow and two other passengers climbed down into it.

The boat capsized in the surf.

The two other passengers survived. Rose Greenhow did not. Her body was recovered on the beach the following morning — weighted down, the accounts agree, by the gold she had insisted on carrying with her when she left the Condor. The gold that had been intended for the Confederate cause had dragged its most effective female intelligence agent to the bottom of the Atlantic.

She was buried with full military honors in Wilmington, North Carolina, draped in a Confederate flag. The women of Wilmington raised a fund for a monument over her grave that stands to this day.

She was forty-seven years old.

How should history assess Rose O'Neal Greenhow?

The question is not straightforward, and the honest answer requires holding two things simultaneously that the commemorative tradition around her has generally preferred to separate.

She was, by any objective measure, one of the most effective intelligence agents of the Civil War — on either side. The network she built from her Washington drawing room, using nothing but her social position and her intelligence, produced intelligence of genuine strategic value at a critical moment in the war's early development. Her transmission of Union plans before Bull Run contributed to a Confederate victory that shaped the entire subsequent course of the conflict. Her continued activity from inside prison demonstrated a professional resourcefulness that would have been admired in any intelligence officer of any era.

She was also fighting for the preservation of a system of human slavery that was among the greatest moral catastrophes in American history. The cause she served with such skill and dedication was a cause built on the ownership of human beings, and the Confederate victory she worked so hard to achieve would have perpetuated that ownership indefinitely. The gold on her wrists when she drowned was Confederate gold — the currency of a government whose constitution explicitly protected slavery as a permanent institution.

These two things — the extraordinary effectiveness and the repugnant cause — cannot be separated without falsifying the history. The Washington socialite who sent battle plans in her courier's hair and kept working from inside a Union prison was serving the same ideology as the plantation owners who worked people to death in the cotton fields of Georgia and Mississippi.

History does not have to choose between acknowledging her effectiveness and acknowledging her cause. It can do both.

That is, in the end, the honest portrait of Rose O'Neal Greenhow — neither the heroine of Confederate memory nor the villain of Union propaganda, but a formidable, brilliant, committed, and morally compromised woman who fought for what she believed in with every tool available to her, and who died for it in the surf off a North Carolina beach with Confederate gold around her neck.

The Torpedo Bureau

Confederate Sabotage and the Birth of Covert Warfare

The retreating army left something behind.

It always does — the detritus of movement, the abandoned equipment, the roads churned to mud by thousands of boots and wagon wheels. Union soldiers advancing up the Virginia Peninsula in the spring of 1862 had learned to read that detritus the way experienced soldiers read any landscape, looking for what was useful and stepping around what wasn't.

They learned to be more careful.

The artillery shell was half-buried in the road, its fuse connected to a pressure plate concealed just beneath the surface. A man stepped on it. The shell detonated. The men around him — who had been advancing up a road, in daylight, in what they had understood to be a relatively secure area behind the Confederate retreat — suddenly understood that the ground itself had become a weapon.

It was, by most accounts, the first time in American military history that soldiers had been killed by what we would today call an improvised explosive device. The weapon had a different name in 1862. They called it a torpedo.

The man who built it was a brigadier general named Gabriel Rains, and what he was building — though neither he nor anyone else fully understood it yet — was the conceptual foundation of modern covert warfare.

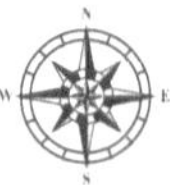

Gabriel James Rains was fifty-eight years old when the Civil War began, a career army officer from North Carolina who had spent decades in the kind of frontier service that left a man with practical knowledge of unconventional problems and unconventional solutions.

He had been thinking about explosive devices for years — not as weapons of terror, exactly, but as force multipliers. A small force defending a position against a larger one needed every advantage the terrain and technology could provide. A buried explosive that detonated under the weight of an advancing soldier was, in Rains's engineering mind, simply an extension of the defensive principle — a way of making ground impassable without requiring a soldier to stand on it.

The Army of the Confederacy gave him the opportunity to test the theory.

When Confederate General Joseph Johnston ordered the withdrawal up the Peninsula in the spring of 1862 — pulling back from Yorktown toward Richmond ahead of McClellan's advancing army — Rains saw his chance. He placed shells along the roads and in the abandoned camps, fused to detonate when stepped on or disturbed. The Union soldiers who encountered them were not prepared for the experience. Nobody was. This was not how war was supposed to work. War had rules — written and unwritten — about what was acceptable and what wasn't, and a weapon that killed men who thought they were walking down a safe road felt, to many on both sides, like a violation of something fundamental.

The reaction was immediate and furious. Union General George McClellan protested formally. Confederate General James Longstreet — Rains's immediate superior — ordered him to stop. The argument that followed went up the Confederate chain of command and produced one of the more revealing debates in the entire war: whether a weapon that was undeniably effective was also undeniably wrong.

Rains was unrepentant. He argued, with the cold logic of a man who had been thinking about this longer than his critics, that a shell buried in the ground was no different in principle from a shell fired from a cannon — both were designed to kill advancing enemy soldiers, and the notion that one was acceptable while the other was monstrous was a distinction without a moral foundation. The soldier killed by a buried shell was just as dead as the soldier killed by artillery, and the Confederate army defending Richmond against a force three times its size needed every tool available.

Jefferson Davis, who had the final word, sided with Rains.

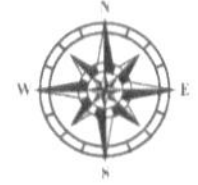

The land mine program that Rains developed from that disputed beginning was, by the standards of its time, sophisticated.

He refined the fusing mechanism — moving from simple pressure plates to more reliable designs that reduced the rate of accidental detonation during placement while maintaining sensitivity to the weight of a man or horse. He developed methods for marking mine locations so that Confederate forces could move through mined areas without becoming casualties of their own weapons — a problem that would bedevil every military that used mines for the next century and a half. He trained officers in emplacement techniques and tactical doctrine for integrating mines into defensive positions.

The results, in the Richmond defenses and later in the defenses of other Confederate cities, were measurable. Union advances slowed in areas where mines were suspected. Casualties were inflicted at points where Confederate conventional forces were too thin to hold the line through firepower alone. The psychological effect — the knowledge that the ground itself might kill you — was a force multiplier that no accounting of actual casualties could fully capture.

Rains also turned his attention to the water.

Underwater mines — which he called torpedoes with the same terminological logic that he applied to land mines — were, if anything, more effective than their buried counterparts. A river or harbor that might contain submerged explosives was a river or harbor that Union naval forces had to approach with extreme caution. The Confederate Navy, which was catastrophically outmatched by the Union's industrial capacity to build warships, could not defeat the Union fleet in conventional naval combat. It could make the waters around Confederate ports and along Confederate rivers dangerous enough to impose costs that a numerically superior enemy could not ignore.

The torpedoes Rains developed for underwater use were anchored below the surface at depths calculated to strike the hulls of passing vessels — detonated by contact fuses that triggered when a ship's hull made contact with the device. The waters around Charleston, Mobile, and the James River approaches to Richmond were seeded with them, and Union naval commanders learned to treat those waters with a respect that their numerical superiority would not otherwise have required.

The most famous moment in Confederate torpedo warfare came at Mobile Bay in August 1864, when the Union monitor Tecumseh struck a Confederate torpedo and sank in minutes, taking most of her crew with her. Admiral David Farragut's response — "Damn the torpedoes, full speed ahead" — has entered American mythology as an expression of aggressive disregard for danger. What it actually expressed was the tactical calculation that stopping in a minefield was more dangerous than moving through one. Farragut was right. The fleet got through. But the Tecumseh was at the bottom of Mobile Bay, and the men who had been aboard her were dead, and Gabriel Rains had put the torpedoes there.

The Confederate Torpedo Bureau that formalized Rains's work into an organizational structure was established in 1862 and expanded steadily as the war ground on and the Confederacy's conventional military options narrowed.

Under the direction of Brigadier General William Norris — who also ran the Confederate Signal Bureau and had a broader conception of unconventional warfare than Rains's engineering focus — the Bureau became something more than a mine-laying operation. It became, in embryo, a special operations organization.

The sabotage campaign that the Bureau directed against Union infrastructure was conducted by agents and operatives rather than uniformed soldiers — men who traveled in civilian clothes, carried false identity documents, and targeted the railways, supply depots, and river vessels that sustained the Union war effort with methods that the laws of war, such as they were, did not clearly address.

The Roanoke River mining operation is among the better-documented Bureau actions — a systematic effort to deny Union naval forces use of the river by seeding it with torpedoes at key points, conducted by Bureau agents working with local Confederate sympathizers who knew the river's depths and currents. The operation achieved its tactical objective. Union gunboats operating on the Roanoke proceeded with a caution that limited their operational effectiveness in ways that the Confederate conventional forces in the region could not have imposed through direct engagement.

The sabotage of Union supply vessels on the Mississippi was conducted by Bureau agents using a variety of methods — devices hidden in coal supplies that were designed to explode when shoveled into furnaces, timed incendiary devices placed in cargo, direct attacks on vessels at unguarded moments. The coal torpedo — a cast-iron device shaped and painted to resemble a lump of coal, filled with black powder — was among the more ingenious Bureau inventions, designed to be mixed into coal supplies at Confederate-sympathetic ports along the river and to detonate when a stoker shoveled it into a ship's furnace. The operational record of the coal torpedo is difficult to reconstruct with precision, but the device is documented in Confederate Bureau records and Union counterintelligence reports of the period.

The Greek Fire attacks on New York City in November 1864 were the most ambitious — and the most revealing — Confederate covert operation of the entire war.

The plan was conceived and executed by a group of Confederate agents operating out of Canada under the broader direction of Jacob Thompson's Montreal operation — the Confederate Secret Service bureau that had been attempting, with mixed results, to conduct covert operations against Northern targets throughout 1864. The New York operation was the most audacious thing they attempted.

The agents — eight men, operating under the command of Lieutenant Colonel Robert Martin — arrived in New York City in November 1864 and checked into hotels across the city under assumed names. Their plan was to set fire to as many hotels simultaneously as possible, creating a conflagration that would spread through the wooden buildings of lower Manhattan and produce the kind of mass civilian panic that the Confederate leadership hoped would force the Union to divert military resources to internal security.

On the night of November 25, 1864, Martin's team moved through the city. Each man carried bottles of Greek Fire — a chemically prepared incendiary compound that ignited spontaneously on contact with air — and each set fires in his assigned hotels before slipping out into the night.

Nineteen hotels were targeted. The fires started in all of them.

None of them burned down.

The Greek Fire compound the agents had been supplied with was defective — either poorly formulated or degraded in transit, it failed to sustain combustion beyond the initial ignition. The hotel fires were discovered and extinguished before they could spread. The conflagration that was supposed to consume lower Manhattan produced instead a series of small fires, a great deal of smoke, and the rapid mobilization of New York's fire department.

The agents fled the city. Most escaped to Canada. Two were eventually captured — one was tried and executed, another imprisoned.

What the operation revealed, in failure, was how close the Confederate covert warfare program had come to crossing a line that the war's other atrocities had not crossed — the deliberate mass killing of Northern civilians in their beds. The hotels that were targeted were full. The plan, if the incendiary compound had worked as intended, would have killed hundreds of people who had no connection to the Union war effort beyond the accident of living in a Northern city.

That it failed was a function of chemistry, not conscience.

Gabriel Rains survived the war and spent his postwar years in Charleston, South Carolina, working as a clerk — the reduction from brigadier general to government clerk being the kind of postwar trajectory that the Confederacy's defeated officers often followed, stripped of the rank and resources that the cause they had served could no longer provide.

He continued to think about mines. He wrote a treatise on torpedo warfare that was, in its way, a remarkably prescient document — anticipating the systematic use of naval mines and land mines in conflicts that would not occur until decades after his death. The weapons he had pioneered at Yorktown in 1862 would kill soldiers in every major conflict of the following century, refined and industrialized beyond anything he had imagined but recognizable in their basic principle as descendants of the shells he had half-buried in the Virginia mud.

He died in 1881, largely forgotten.

The Torpedo Bureau he had helped create was, in retrospect, one of the more significant military innovations of the Civil War — not for the specific damage it inflicted, which was real but limited, but for what it represented. The deliberate targeting of infrastructure. The use of civilian-clothed agents to conduct military operations. The employment of incendiary and explosive devices against targets beyond the conventional battlefield. The attempt to bring the war to the enemy's cities and supply lines through means that conventional military force could not achieve.

These were not new ideas in the abstract. Armies had always tried to disrupt enemy supply lines and demoralize enemy populations. What the Confederate Torpedo Bureau did was begin to systematize those impulses — to build an organizational structure, develop specialized equipment, train dedicated operatives, and direct them against specific targets with specific objectives.

Modern special operations forces would recognize the doctrine. They would recognize the problems too — the defective equipment, the compromised agents, the gap between what covert operations promised and what they delivered. Those problems were not Confederate inventions. They were the permanent features of a kind of warfare that the Torpedo Bureau had helped bring into being.

The shells buried in the Virginia road. The torpedoes anchored in the Mobile Bay channel. The bottles of Greek Fire carried through the corridors of New York hotels.

The Confederacy lost the war. The weapons survived it.

The Signal Man of Bull Run

Edward Porter Alexander's Finest Hour

He was twenty-six years old and he was watching through a telescope when he saw something that changed the battle.

The hill they had assigned him — Signal Hill, on the Confederate left flank overlooking the Bull Run battlefield — gave him a view that nobody on the ground possessed. Below him, obscured by the terrain and the smoke of the morning's fighting, Confederate infantry were holding a line that was being pressed from the front. What Alexander could see from his elevation that the men on the line could not was what was happening to their left.

Union troops. A column of them, moving along a road that would bring them around the Confederate flank before anyone below realized the movement was underway.

He reached for his flags.

What happened in the next few minutes — the message sent, the warning received, the Confederate response that met the flanking movement before it could develop — is one of the most debated small moments in Civil War military history. Was Alexander's signal decisive? Did it save the Confederate left? Did it change the outcome of the battle that would become the first great shock of the war?

Alexander himself believed it did. He said so for the rest of his life, with the quiet confidence of a man who had been there and knew what he had seen.

The historians have been arguing about it ever since.

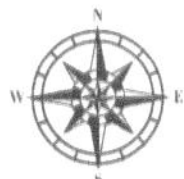

Edward Porter Alexander grew up in Washington, Georgia, the son of a prosperous banker, and arrived at West Point in 1853 with the academic ability and competitive instincts that the Academy rewarded. He graduated third in his class in 1857 — an achievement that in the antebellum army opened doors that middle-of-the-class graduates could not access — and was assigned to the Corps of Engineers, which was where the Army put its best technical minds.

The assignment that shaped everything that followed came in 1859, when Alexander was detailed to work with Albert Myer on the development of the wig-wag signal system. He was twenty-four years old, technically brilliant, and genuinely interested in the communication problem that Myer had been working on for years. He learned the system thoroughly — the binary code, the telescope work, the station selection and preparation, the operational procedures for integrating signal communication into battlefield command. He was, by Myer's own assessment, one of the best students he had trained.

Two years later, when Virginia seceded and Alexander resigned his commission to join the Confederacy, he took everything Myer had taught him with him.

There is something almost poignant about this, viewed from a distance of a century and a half — the teacher's system turned against the teacher's army, the student's training becoming the instrument of the student's former comrades' defeat. Alexander never expressed any particular guilt about it. He was a Georgian. His state had left the Union. He left with it. The signal system he had learned in the Union Army was a tool, and tools belonged to whoever was skilled enough to use them.

He was very skilled.

The morning of July 21, 1861, found Alexander on Signal Hill with his telescope and his flags and a commanding view of a battlefield that was about to become the site of the first major shock of the American Civil War.

The Confederate position at Bull Run was strong in the center and on the right but thinner on the left — a weakness that Union General Irvin McDowell had identified in his operational planning and intended to exploit. The Union flanking movement that McDowell ordered — a column swinging wide to the west to come around the Confederate left — was, on paper, the kind of tactical maneuver that could collapse a defensive line before it could be reinforced.

On paper. In practice, there was Alexander on his hill with his telescope.

He saw the Union column moving. He saw where it was going. He understood, with the tactical clarity that his West Point training had given him, what it meant for the Confederate left if that movement was allowed to develop unopposed. And he sent a message.

The text of the message, as Alexander later recorded it, was: "Look out for your left, your position is turned."

It was received by Captain E.P. Jones at the Confederate signal station, relayed to Confederate commanders, and — in Alexander's account and in Beauregard's postwar memoir — acted upon. Troops were shifted. The flanking movement was met. The Confederate left held.

That is Alexander's version. It is supported by Beauregard's account and by the basic facts of what happened on the battlefield that day — the Union flanking movement was detected and countered, the Confederate left held long enough for Johnston's reinforcements to arrive from the Shenandoah Valley, and the battle eventually turned into the Confederate victory that sent Union forces and Washington civilians fleeing together down the roads toward the capital.

The historical debate is about causation, not about the facts.

Some historians — examining the timing of Confederate troop movements, the distances involved, and the orders that Confederate commanders issued in the hours before Alexander's signal — have argued that the redeployment of Confederate forces to meet the Union flanking movement was already underway before Alexander's message arrived. That Confederate commanders had independently identified the threat and were responding to it. That Alexander's signal confirmed what was already known rather than revealing what was not.

Alexander, when he encountered this argument in postwar historical discussions, disputed it with the patience of a man who felt he was being deprived of something he had earned. He had seen the movement. He had sent the warning. The Confederate left had held. The connection between those three facts seemed self-evident to him.

Whether it was decisive or merely confirmatory, the signal was real. The movement was detected. The battle went the way it went.

Bull Run made Alexander's reputation and opened the door to the career that followed — a career that would take him from signal officer to artillery commander to one of the most analytically gifted military minds the Confederacy produced.

He was given command of an artillery battalion and proved at it what his West Point record had suggested he would prove at almost anything he attempted: that he was very good. Confederate artillery in the war's early period was poorly organized, inadequately trained, and doctrinally incoherent — the guns were there, but the systematic thinking about how to use them most effectively had not been developed. Alexander helped develop it.

He organized his battalion with the methodical thoroughness that characterized everything he did — standardizing training, developing fire coordination procedures, thinking carefully about the relationship between artillery and infantry in ways that the Confederate Army had not previously institutionalized. The results were visible in the battles where his guns were engaged. Alexander's artillery was consistently more effective than the Confederate average, not because his guns were better but because his doctrine was clearer.

By Gettysburg in July 1863 he was the artillery commander for Longstreet's First Corps — the officer responsible for the most consequential artillery operation of the entire war.

The artillery bombardment that preceded Pickett's Charge on July 3, 1863, was Alexander's most visible moment and his most painful one.

He had been given a task that was, from the beginning, probably impossible — to suppress the Union artillery on Cemetery Ridge sufficiently that Pickett's division and the supporting infantry could cross the open ground between Seminary Ridge and Cemetery Ridge without being destroyed. Nearly fifteen thousand Confederate soldiers would make that crossing. The ground they had to cover was three-quarters of a mile of open farmland under the guns of the strongest artillery position the Union Army had established during the battle.

Alexander massed his guns — approximately 160 Confederate artillery pieces, the largest concentration of artillery the Confederacy assembled during the war — and opened fire at one in the afternoon on July 3. The bombardment that followed was, in terms of sheer noise and physical spectacle, the most impressive artillery display of the entire conflict. It shook the ground for miles. It was heard in Washington.

It did not achieve its objective.

The Union artillery on Cemetery Ridge was not suppressed. It was conserved — pulled back from the ridge line, its ammunition husbanded for the infantry assault that Union commanders knew was coming. When Confederate ammunition began to run low and Alexander sent word to Pickett that if he was going to advance he needed to do so immediately, the Union guns that had apparently fallen silent were waiting.

Alexander knew, as he watched Pickett's division begin its advance, that something was wrong. He could see that the Union artillery had not been adequately suppressed. He sent a message to Longstreet suggesting a delay. Longstreet — who had opposed the entire assault from the beginning and was executing it under orders he believed were mistaken — did not stop it.

Alexander watched what happened next from his position on Seminary Ridge. He watched fifteen thousand men walk into the fire of guns that should have been silenced and weren't. He watched the advance that was supposed to break the Union center break instead against it. He watched the men who came back — fewer than half of those who had gone forward.

He never forgot it. How could he.

The postwar memoir that Alexander published in 1907 — *Military Memoirs of a Confederate* — is one of the most remarkable documents produced by any participant in the Civil War, on either side.

Most Confederate memoirs of the period were exercises in retrospective justification — the Lost Cause narrative that transformed Confederate defeat into noble tragedy, attributed the loss to overwhelming Northern numbers and resources rather than to Confederate strategic or tactical failures, and declined to examine too carefully the decisions that had led to the outcome. They were, in many cases, acts of motivated historical blindness.

Alexander's memoir was the opposite.

He examined Confederate strategy with a clarity that made some of his surviving comrades uncomfortable. He assessed Confederate tactical decisions — including decisions he had been part of — with an honesty that did not spare himself or the commanders he had served. He wrote about Pickett's Charge with the analytical rigor of a man who had thought about those three-quarters of a mile of open ground for forty years and had arrived at conclusions he was not going to soften to spare anyone's feelings.

He concluded that the Confederacy had lost the war not primarily because of Northern numerical and industrial superiority — though those advantages were real — but because of strategic and tactical decisions that had squandered Confederate strengths and compounded Confederate weaknesses. The decision to fight the kind of offensive war that consumed irreplaceable Confederate manpower in frontal assaults was, in Alexander's assessment, the central mistake. The Confederacy should have fought defensively, making the North pay so high a price for offensive operations that Northern political will would eventually collapse.

It was, and remains, one of the most cogent analyses of Confederate strategic failure ever written. It was also, coming from a man who had fought throughout the war with complete commitment to the Confederate cause, an act of intellectual honesty that the Lost Cause tradition neither expected nor welcomed.

Alexander had been right about the Union flanking movement at Bull Run. He had been right about Pickett's Charge before it started. He was right, in his postwar analysis, about why the Confederacy lost.

Being right, in all three cases, was not enough to change the outcome.

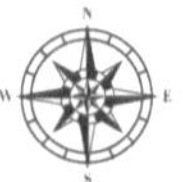

Edward Porter Alexander lived until 1910 — long enough to see the war he had fought recede into history, to watch the veterans of both sides grow old together at reunions that the passage of time had made possible, to observe the transformation of the conflict from lived experience into mythology.

He taught at West Point after the war. He worked in railroad management and as an arbitrator in international disputes — the analytical mind that had organized Confederate artillery finding new problems to organize. He wrote his memoir at the end of a long life, at seventy-two, from the distance that the years provided.

The signal on the hill at Bull Run was forty-six years in the past when he finished writing. He still believed it had mattered. He still described it with the specificity of a man recalling something he had seen yesterday — the Union column moving through his telescope, the flags in his hands, the message going out across the valley.

Look out for your left. Your position is turned.

Whether it saved the Confederate left or merely confirmed what Confederate commanders were already discovering for themselves is a question the historical record cannot definitively resolve. What the record does establish is that Alexander was there, that he saw what he saw, that he sent what he sent, and that the Confederate left held.

The rest is argument. And argument, as Alexander well understood, was what soldiers did after the fighting was over, when the flags were put away and the only weapons left were words on a page.

He was good at that too.

The Canadian Connection

Confederate Secret Service Operations in the North

Jacob Thompson arrived in Montreal in the spring of 1864 with several million dollars in Confederate gold and an assignment that would have tested the capabilities of a far more experienced intelligence officer than he was.

Thompson was sixty-three years old, a Mississippi politician of considerable distinction — former congressman, former Secretary of the Interior under President Buchanan, a man whose career had been built in the drawing rooms and legislative chambers of Washington rather than in the field. He was not a spy. He had never run an intelligence operation. He had never managed agents or planned covert actions or navigated the particular moral and operational complexities of a secret war conducted on neutral territory.

Jefferson Davis sent him anyway, because the Confederacy was running out of options and Thompson was available and trusted, and sometimes that has to be enough.

The mission Davis gave him was breathtaking in its ambition and vague in its specifics: go to Canada, make contact with the Confederate sympathizer networks in the American Midwest, spend the gold, and do whatever could be done to destabilize the Northern war effort sufficiently to force a negotiated peace before the 1864 presidential election gave Lincoln a mandate to see the war through to its conclusion.

Thompson set up his headquarters in Montreal, established a secondary base in Toronto, and began making contact with the networks his predecessor had been cultivating — the Copperhead organizations, the secret societies of Confederate sympathizers that claimed hundreds of thousands of members across Ohio, Indiana, and Illinois, the Sons of Liberty and the Order of American Knights and the various other organizations that had been promising, for months, that the Midwest was ready to rise.

It was not ready to rise. It was barely ready to meet.

The Northwest Conspiracy was the most ambitious operation Thompson attempted and the one that most clearly illustrated the gap between Confederate intelligence ambitions and Confederate intelligence capabilities.

The plan, in its fullest conception, was extraordinary — a coordinated uprising across the Midwestern states timed to coincide with the Democratic National Convention in Chicago in August 1864, where the peace wing of the Democratic Party was expected to nominate a candidate on a platform that would effectively end the war on terms favorable to the Confederacy. The uprising would liberate Confederate prisoners held at Camp Douglas outside Chicago and at other prison camps across the Midwest — releasing tens of thousands of Confederate soldiers who would be armed and would provide the military backbone of the insurrection. Simultaneously, Confederate agents would seize federal arsenals, cut telegraph lines, destroy railway bridges, and create enough chaos across Ohio, Indiana, and Illinois that the Lincoln government would be forced to divert military resources from the front to deal with the internal crisis.

If it had worked, it might have changed the war.

It did not work. It did not come close to working. And the reasons it did not work reveal almost everything important about the Confederate covert operations program's fundamental limitations.

The first problem was the Copperhead organizations themselves. Thompson had been told, and had believed, that the Sons of Liberty had somewhere between 300,000 and 500,000 members across the Midwest — a figure that its leader, Clement Vallandigham, had provided with the enthusiasm of a man who had a strong interest in appearing more powerful than he was. The actual number of members willing to take up arms against the federal government was, it turned out, considerably smaller. When Thompson's agents began making concrete operational requests — specific commitments, specific dates, specific numbers of men who would show up with weapons when the signal came — the answers they received were consistently disappointing.

The members of the Northwest Conspiracy were, for the most part, men who were opposed to the war and willing to say so in lodge meetings. They were not, in anything like sufficient numbers, men who were prepared to commit treason with firearms in their hands.

The second problem was Union counterintelligence.

Colonel Henry Carrington, the Union officer responsible for military security across the Midwest, had been watching the Copperhead organizations and the Confederate agents moving among them for months before Thompson arrived in Canada. His intelligence network had penetrated the Sons of Liberty at multiple levels. He had informers in the lodge meetings. He had agents in communication with Thompson's operatives. He was, in many cases, reading Confederate operational communications almost as quickly as the intended recipients.

When Thompson's agents finalized their plans for the August uprising — the specific dates, the specific targets, the specific coordination with the prisoner liberation operations — Carrington knew about it. When the Confederate agents arrived in Chicago for the Democratic Convention, Union counterintelligence officers were there too, watching, documenting, waiting.

The uprising was supposed to begin on August 29, 1864, timed to the convention's opening. It did not begin. The Confederate agents who arrived in Chicago found a city that was far more heavily garrisoned than their intelligence had suggested, Copperhead leaders who suddenly developed cold feet when confronted with the actual moment of commitment, and the general atmosphere of an operation that had been compromised before it started.

The convention nominated George McClellan on a peace platform, as expected. McClellan, to the considerable frustration of the peace wing that had nominated him, promptly repudiated the peace plank and ran as a war Democrat. Lincoln won the election in November. The Northwest Conspiracy produced exactly nothing except a collection of Union intelligence files that documented the operation in embarrassing detail.

Thompson tried again in November, with the Camp Douglas liberation plot — a revised version of the August plan that was similarly penetrated by Union intelligence and similarly abandoned when the Confederate agents arrived to find that the operation had been compromised. The Confederate prisoners at Camp Douglas remained in Camp Douglas. The uprising did not happen.

The gold Thompson had brought from Richmond was disappearing into operations that produced no results, agents who took Confederate money and delivered Confederate nothing, and the general overhead of maintaining a covert operations base in a neutral country whose government was increasingly uncomfortable with what was happening on its territory.

The St. Albans Raid of October 1864 was a departure from the conspiracy-and-insurrection model of Thompson's earlier operations — smaller in ambition, more concrete in execution, and ultimately more successful at achieving its tactical objectives while failing completely at its strategic ones.

St. Albans was a small Vermont town about fifteen miles from the Canadian border — quiet, prosperous, and entirely unprepared for what arrived on October 19, 1864.

Twenty-two Confederate raiders, led by Lieutenant Bennett Young, had crossed the border from Canada in small groups over the preceding days, checking into St. Albans hotels as ordinary travelers. On the afternoon of the 19th they assembled in the town square, produced their weapons, announced that St. Albans was now under Confederate military occupation, and proceeded to rob three banks simultaneously.

The operation had a certain audacious style. Young's men moved efficiently through the three banks, collecting approximately $208,000 in cash — a significant sum, though less than the $300,000 that some accounts claim — while a smaller group attempted to set fire to the town using bottles of Greek Fire similar to those that would be used, with similar lack of success, in the New York hotel attacks the following month. The fires mostly didn't take. One townsman was killed when he attempted to resist. The raiders rode north for the Canadian border with their stolen money and crossed it before Union forces could organize an effective pursuit.

In Canada, they were arrested by Canadian authorities — and then released, and then re-arrested, and then released again, in a legal and diplomatic tangle that dragged on for months and produced, in the end, no extradition and no meaningful accountability for the raiders. The stolen money was partially returned, in amounts that various sources report differently. Bennett Young went back to the Confederacy.

The diplomatic fallout between the United States and Britain — Canada was still a British dominion — was significant and lasted well beyond the war's end. The British government, already under American pressure over the Confederate commerce raiders that had been built in British shipyards, found itself dealing with additional American anger over the St. Albans affair. The relationship between the two countries, never entirely comfortable during the war years, became more strained.

This was, presumably, something the Confederacy counted as a success — driving a wedge between the United States and Britain was a component of Confederate strategic thinking throughout the war. Whether the St. Albans Raid materially advanced that goal, or whether it merely created diplomatic irritation without strategic consequence, is difficult to assess. What is clear is that robbing Vermont banks did not cause Britain to recognize the Confederacy, which was the outcome that Confederate strategy actually required.

Why did the Canadian operations fail so consistently?

The question deserves a direct answer, because the failures were not accidental — they were the predictable results of structural problems that no amount of gold or operational creativity could overcome.

The first problem was strategic impossibility. The goal of the Canadian operations — forcing a negotiated peace through internal destabilization of the Northern states — required a level of Copperhead organization, commitment, and military capability that never existed. Thompson had been told it existed. He had wanted to believe it existed. The Confederate leadership in Richmond had needed to believe it existed, because the alternative — accepting that there was no viable path to victory except on the battlefield, where the news was consistently bad — was too bleak to contemplate.

The intelligence Thompson's operation produced about its own capabilities was systematically optimistic, because the people providing that intelligence — the Copperhead leaders, the Confederate sympathizers, the men who were taking Confederate gold — had strong incentives to tell Thompson what he wanted to hear. A Sons of Liberty chapter that claimed 10,000 members received Confederate money and Confederate attention. A chapter that admitted it had 200 members who would probably not show up when it mattered received nothing. The incentive structure produced inflated figures and false confidence, and Thompson, who was not an experienced intelligence officer, did not have the professional skepticism to discount them appropriately.

The second problem was Union counterintelligence. Carrington's operation in the Midwest was genuinely effective — better resourced, better organized, and better at penetrating the Confederate networks than the Confederate operations were at detecting the penetration. Thompson suspected, by the autumn of 1864, that some of his operations had been compromised. He was not wrong. He lacked the ability to identify which agents had been turned and which had not, which meant he lacked the ability to trust any of them completely.

The third problem was the agents themselves. Some of them were genuinely capable — Bennett Young's St. Albans raiders were disciplined and well-organized by the standards of the Canadian operation. Others were not. The New York hotel fire plot drew on agents whose tradecraft was poor, whose incendiary materials were defective, and whose planning had not adequately addressed the question of what happened if the fires didn't spread as expected.

They didn't spread. The hotels didn't burn. The men who set the fires mostly escaped. The operation produced, beyond the initial alarm and a great deal of smoke, nothing.

Jacob Thompson left Canada in early 1865 and made his way to Europe, where he spent several years in exile before eventually returning to the United States. He was never prosecuted for his role in the Canadian operations — the evidence against him, though substantial, was entangled in the diplomatic complications of operations conducted on neutral territory, and the postwar political climate was not conducive to the lengthy legal proceedings his prosecution would have required.

He returned to Mississippi and to a version of his prewar life — reduced in circumstances, as most Confederate leaders were reduced, but present and functional in ways that the men who had actually fought in the Confederate Army often were not, having survived the war without having been in it in the conventional sense.

He maintained, in his postwar writings and statements, that the Canadian operations had been sound in conception if not in execution — that the Copperhead networks had been real, that the opportunities had existed, that better luck or better agents or better timing might have produced different results.

Perhaps. The honest assessment is simpler. The Confederate Secret Service Bureau sent an inexperienced politician with a suitcase full of gold to a foreign country and asked him to foment a revolution in the American Midwest. The revolution didn't happen because it couldn't happen — because the conditions that would have been necessary for it to happen did not exist, and no amount of Confederate gold was going to create them.

The Confederacy was losing the war on the battlefield. It was not going to win it in the hotel rooms of Montreal.

The Lady in the Saddle

Belle Boyd and the Art of Battlefield Intelligence

She was seventeen years old when she shot a Union soldier.

The details of the incident — July 4, 1861, Martinsburg, Virginia, the first Independence Day of the war — were not disputed, then or later. A group of Union soldiers had come to the Boyd family home to raise a Federal flag over it, which was the kind of thing Union soldiers did in the first weeks of the occupation of northern Virginia, and which the families whose houses were being used as flag poles received with varying degrees of accommodation. The Boyds did not accommodate.

Words were exchanged. A soldier — drunk, by most accounts, though the specific degree of his intoxication has been reported differently across different sources — spoke to Belle Boyd's mother in terms that Belle Boyd found unacceptable. She went upstairs, came back with a pistol, and shot him.

He didn't die. The wound was described as serious but not fatal, and the Union Army's subsequent investigation concluded that the circumstances justified no prosecution — a remarkable degree of leniency that reflected either genuine sympathy for the provocation or a practical recognition that prosecuting a seventeen-year-old girl for shooting a drunk soldier would generate more trouble than it was worth.

Belle Boyd drew her own conclusions from the incident. She had acted. There had been no serious consequences. The Yankees could be managed.

It was, in retrospect, a dangerous lesson to learn at seventeen. She spent the next four years testing its limits.

The intelligence operation that Belle Boyd built in Martinsburg was not, by the standards of professional intelligence work, particularly sophisticated. It did not need to be. The raw material was already there.

Her family ran a hotel. Union officers stayed in it. Union officers talked — at dinner, in the parlor, in the comfortable assumption that the pretty daughter of the house was a social fixture rather than a security concern. Belle Boyd listened. She had a quick mind, a good memory, and the particular social intelligence of someone who had grown up in a household where the management of guests was a professional skill. She understood how to make people comfortable. Comfortable people talked more than they should.

What she heard, she passed on. The methods were various — notes carried by couriers, messages passed through a network of trusted locals, occasional direct contact with Confederate officers when the military situation brought Confederate forces close enough to make direct communication possible. The intelligence she provided was tactical rather than strategic — troop positions, unit movements, the disposition of Union forces in the Shenandoah Valley — but tactical intelligence in the right place at the right time was exactly what Stonewall Jackson needed as he conducted the brilliant Valley Campaign of 1862 that would become one of the most studied military operations in American history.

Jackson's Valley Campaign was a masterpiece of deception, speed, and aggressive action — a small Confederate force tying down Union troops many times its size through a combination of rapid movement and aggressive attack that kept the Union commanders in the valley perpetually off-balance. The intelligence network that supported it drew on multiple sources, and Belle Boyd was one of them — not the only one, and not always the most important one, but a real and documented contributor to a campaign that changed the war in the eastern theater.

She was arrested for the first time in the summer of 1861, questioned, and released — the authorities deciding that the evidence against her was insufficient to sustain a prosecution and that imprisoning her would create more complications than it resolved. She went back to collecting intelligence. She was arrested again. Released again. The pattern repeated with a regularity that suggested either that Union counterintelligence was genuinely unable to build a sustainable case against her or that the authorities were reluctant to treat a young woman of good family with the seriousness that her actual activities warranted.

Both things were probably true.

The First Battle of Front Royal on May 23, 1862, is the episode on which Belle Boyd's historical reputation primarily rests — and it deserves examination with the care that any dramatic story demands, separating what the documentary record establishes from what subsequent accounts have embellished.

What is documented: Jackson's forces were approaching Front Royal, a small Virginia town held by a Union garrison. Belle Boyd was in Front Royal, staying at the house of a relative. She had been gathering intelligence about the Union garrison's strength and dispositions — information that she understood would be valuable to Jackson's advancing forces.

What she did with that intelligence is where the story becomes both dramatic and contested.

Boyd's own account — given in her 1865 memoir and in numerous subsequent interviews over a long postwar career — describes her running across an open field under Union fire to reach Confederate advance skirmishers and deliver her intelligence in person. She had been unable to send a courier, she explained, because the situation was developing too rapidly and the information was too time-sensitive to wait. So she ran.

The image is extraordinary — a young woman in a dress, crossing open ground, Union soldiers firing at her, Confederate skirmishers watching in astonishment as she approached their line waving her bonnet and calling out information about Union positions.

Confederate officers who were present at Front Royal confirmed, in postwar accounts, that Boyd had appeared during the action and provided information about Union dispositions. Stonewall Jackson sent her a note after the battle — which she kept and which she quoted in her memoir — thanking her for the service she had rendered and confirming that her intelligence had been useful.

The specific details — the open-field run, the Union fire, the bonnet-waving — rest primarily on Boyd's own testimony, which was consistent across multiple tellings but which she had every reason to present in the most dramatic possible light. Boyd was, by the end of the war and increasingly as the years passed, a professional celebrity of the Lost Cause — someone whose story was her livelihood, and whose livelihood depended on the story remaining dramatic.

Historians have generally accepted the core of the account — that Boyd provided useful intelligence at Front Royal, that she did so at some personal risk, and that her information contributed to Jackson's success in capturing the town and its Union garrison — while treating the specific dramatic details with appropriate caution.

Jackson took Front Royal. The Union garrison was captured. Boyd's contribution was real, whatever its precise form.

The arrests that followed Front Royal were less gentlemanly than the earlier ones.

Union counterintelligence, now fully aware of Boyd's activities and no longer inclined to dismiss her as a harmless young woman, arrested her in July 1862 and transported her to the Old Capitol Prison in Washington — the same facility that had held Rose Greenhow. Boyd's imprisonment there lasted about a month before she was released in a prisoner exchange and sent south into Confederate territory.

She went back to spying. The Confederacy was not, in 1862, inclined to waste an asset simply because it had been temporarily compromised.

The second imprisonment came in 1863 — again the Old Capitol Prison, again a period of confinement that Boyd experienced as an opportunity for the kind of theatrical resistance that she had by now developed into an art form. She sang Confederate songs loudly enough that they could be heard in the street. She hung a Confederate flag from her window until it was confiscated. She charmed her guards, conducted conversations with visitors that she later claimed contained encoded information, and generally behaved with the cheerful defiance of someone who had concluded that the worst the Union would do to her was imprison her again, which they had already done twice.

She was right. They released her again.

The third and final major disruption of Boyd's Confederate career came in 1864, when she was placed on a blockade runner and exiled to England — a solution that effectively removed her from the operational theater while avoiding the political complications of prosecuting her yet again.

The blockade runner was intercepted by a Union naval vessel. And this is where Belle Boyd's story takes its most remarkable turn — because the Union officer assigned to escort her to Canada, from where she would make her way to England, was a young naval officer named Samuel Hardinge.

He fell in love with her.

She married him.

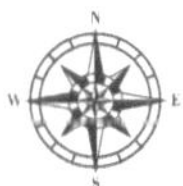

The marriage of Belle Boyd and Samuel Hardinge is one of the more improbable personal stories of the entire war — the Confederate spy and the Union officer assigned to guard her, married within months of their first meeting, Hardinge resigning his commission and following her to England where she had gone to write her memoir and give lectures about her wartime adventures.

The marriage did not survive the war. Hardinge returned to the United States, was arrested by Union authorities for his apparent Confederate sympathies — an irony that would be almost comic if it weren't genuinely damaging to the man involved — and died shortly after the war's end under circumstances that have never been fully established. Boyd was widowed at twenty-two.

She married twice more. She went on the stage. She gave lectures across the United States and Britain, telling the story of her wartime adventures to audiences who paid to hear it, refining and dramatizing as professional necessity required. The specific incidents grew more colorful with each retelling. The open-field run at Front Royal became more dramatic each time she described it.

By the end of the nineteenth century, Belle Boyd had become one of the most famous women of the Civil War — not because of the intelligence value of what she had actually done, which was real but limited, but because of the story she told about it, which was irresistible.

She died in 1900, in Kilbourn, Wisconsin, of a heart attack, while on a lecture tour. She was fifty-six years old. The local Grand Army of the Republic post — Union veterans — provided an honor guard at her funeral, because whatever she had done during the war, she had done it with a kind of style that even her former enemies found it difficult not to admire.

The historical Belle Boyd — as distinct from the legendary one she spent her postwar life constructing — is a figure who requires both acknowledgment and proportion.

She was a real intelligence asset for the Confederacy in the early part of the war, operating in the Shenandoah Valley at a time and in a place where her social access and her willingness to take risks produced information that Confederate commanders found useful. The Front Royal incident happened in some form, and her contribution to Jackson's success there was recognized by Jackson himself.

She was also, from the beginning, as much a performer as an operative — someone who understood instinctively that her value to the Confederate cause was not limited to the intelligence she collected but extended to the image she projected and the story she told. The shooting of the Union soldier on the Fourth of July was a genuinely impulsive act. Everything that followed had, increasingly, the quality of a performance — calculated, audience-aware, shaped by a young woman who understood that she was becoming famous and who was not displeased by the discovery.

The Union Army's persistent failure to deal with her effectively was partly a function of the genuine evidentiary difficulties of prosecuting intelligence cases, and partly a function of the social assumptions about women that made it difficult for Union officers to take her seriously as a security threat until she had demonstrated, repeatedly and at considerable cost, that she was one.

She exploited those assumptions brilliantly. It was, perhaps, the most sophisticated thing she did.

The Lady in the Saddle — the image she cultivated, the persona she performed, the legend she built across four decades of lectures and memoirs — was a construction as deliberate and as effective as any cipher Rose Greenhow had written or any signal Edward Alexander had sent. Belle Boyd understood, before most people of her time understood it, that the story of a thing could be as powerful as the thing itself.

She told her story for forty years, to anyone who would pay to hear it.

They kept paying.

The Copperhead Networks

Confederate Sympathizers in the Northern States

T he war was not universally popular in the North.

This is one of those historical facts that the triumphalist narrative of the Civil War tends to smooth over — the clean story of Union against Confederacy, freedom against slavery, the right side against the wrong one, obscuring the messier reality that a substantial portion of the Northern population had serious reservations about the conflict, its conduct, its costs, and its aims. By 1862 those reservations had hardened, in certain quarters, into organized political opposition. By 1863 that opposition had a name that its enemies had given it, intending contempt, and that it had, in some cases, adopted with a defiance that said something about the mood of the people wearing it.

Copperheads. Named for the snake that strikes without warning. Some of them cut the copper Liberty heads from pennies and wore them as lapel pins — reclaiming the insult, turning it into a badge.

They were not a monolithic movement. They were not all traitors, though some of them were. They were not all Confederate agents, though some of them cooperated with Confederate agents. They were, at their broadest, a coalition of people who opposed the war for reasons that ranged from principled constitutional objection to naked racism to simple exhaustion with a conflict that was killing people at a rate that 1861's optimism had not anticipated and 1863's reality could not ignore.

Understanding them requires resisting the temptation to flatten them — to accept either the Confederate propaganda that portrayed them as a vast and powerful fifth column ready to rise against the Lincoln government, or the Union propaganda that portrayed them as traitors to a man. The truth was more complicated and, in its complexity, more interesting than either version.

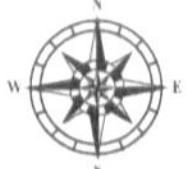

The political geography of the Midwest in 1861 was not what later generations would assume it to be.

The states of Ohio, Indiana, and Illinois had been settled in large part by migrants from the upper South — Kentucky, Tennessee, Virginia — who had brought with them cultural ties, family connections, and in some cases political sympathies that did not map neatly onto the Union-Confederate binary that the war was imposing on the country. These were not slaveholders, for the most part. The economy of the southern Midwest was not a slave economy. But they had cousins across the Ohio River. They had grown up in a world where the South was not a foreign country but a neighbor, and the war asked them to treat it as an enemy.

Some of them couldn't.

The Democratic Party in the Midwest had been, before the war, the party of Jacksonian democracy — skeptical of federal power, suspicious of New England reform movements, culturally conservative in ways that made the abolitionist wing of the Republican Party feel alien and threatening. When Lincoln issued the Emancipation Proclamation in January 1863, transforming the war's stated purpose from the preservation of the Union to the abolition of slavery, a significant portion of the Midwestern Democratic base concluded that this was not the war they had signed up for.

The Emancipation Proclamation did not make these men Confederate sympathizers. It made them war opponents — which was a different thing, though the distinction was not always observed by the Union military authorities who were arresting people for expressing antiwar sentiments in 1862 and 1863.

Clement Vallandigham was the most prominent figure in this world — an Ohio congressman whose opposition to the war was principled, consistent, and expressed with a rhetorical force that made him either a champion of civil liberties or a treasonous obstructionist depending on whose account you read. He argued, with genuine constitutional grounding, that Lincoln's suspension of habeas corpus was illegal, that the arrest of civilians by military tribunals was unconstitutional, and that the war itself was a catastrophic mistake that should be ended through negotiated peace.

In May 1863, Union General Ambrose Burnside — who had his own complicated relationship with catastrophic mistakes, having commanded the Army of the Potomac at Fredericksburg — had Vallandigham arrested for making a speech that violated a military order against expressing sympathy for the enemy. He was tried by a military commission, convicted, and sentenced to imprisonment.

Lincoln, who understood the political dynamics better than Burnside did, commuted the sentence to banishment — sending Vallandigham to Confederate lines, from where he eventually made his way to Canada and then back to Ohio, where he ran for governor in 1863 on a peace platform and lost, though not by the margin the Republicans had hoped.

The Vallandigham episode illustrated everything that was complicated about the Copperhead question. He was not a Confederate agent. He did not provide Confederate intelligence services with information. He opposed the war on constitutional grounds that were not, in themselves, indefensible. And yet his rhetoric provided political cover for people who were doing things considerably more concrete than making speeches, and his network of contacts extended into organizations whose relationship with Confederate intelligence was considerably less ambiguous than his own.

The Knights of the Golden Circle was the most significant of the secret societies that flourished in the Midwest during the war years — and also the most difficult to assess accurately, because its membership figures, its organizational coherence, and its actual capabilities were systematically exaggerated by everyone who had an interest in the exaggeration.

The organization had been founded before the war by a Cincinnati physician named George Bickley, with the original aim of promoting American expansion into Mexico and Central America — the "golden circle" of the title referring to a geographic area centered on Havana that would, in Bickley's vision, become a great slave empire extending from the American South through the Caribbean and into Latin America. The vision was grandiose and the organization that promoted it was, in the prewar years, more fraternal lodge than political movement — men who liked rituals and secret handshakes and the feeling of belonging to something important.

The war transformed it. The Knights of the Golden Circle became, in the Midwest of 1862 and 1863, a vehicle for antiwar sentiment and, in some cases, for more concrete forms of resistance to the Union war effort. It reorganized itself as the Order of American Knights in 1863 and then as the Sons of Liberty in 1864, each reorganization claiming to purge the corruption and inefficiency of the previous structure while maintaining the essential character of a secret society whose members were opposed to the Lincoln administration and sympathetic, in varying degrees, to the Confederate cause.

The membership figures that the organization claimed — and that Confederate agents like Jacob Thompson accepted with insufficient skepticism — were extraordinary. Vallandigham, who became the Supreme Commander of the Sons of Liberty after his return from exile, claimed 300,000 members in Ohio, Indiana, and Illinois alone. Some estimates ran higher.

The actual number of members who would have taken up arms against the federal government was a fraction of this — a small fraction, as the failure of the Northwest Conspiracy had demonstrated with embarrassing clarity.

Historians who have examined the Knights and its successor organizations most carefully — including Frank Klement, whose revisionist scholarship on the Copperhead movement has been influential if not universally accepted — have argued that the organizations were, in operational terms, largely hollow. The rituals were real. The meetings were real. The antiwar sentiment was real. The capacity for organized military action was not.

Klement's argument — that the Copperhead threat was substantially manufactured by Union military authorities who had political and institutional reasons to portray antiwar dissent as treason — is important and deserves to be taken seriously. The Union military commission system that prosecuted Copperhead cases was not a neutral arbiter of evidence.

The charges of conspiracy that were brought against Copperhead leaders were, in several documented cases, based on evidence that was exaggerated, fabricated, or both.

The problem with Klement's revisionism is that it goes too far in the opposite direction. The organizations were real. The Confederate contact was real. Some members of the Knights and its successors did provide Confederate agents with intelligence, logistical support, and political cover that had genuine operational value. The question is not whether the Copperhead networks existed and had Confederate connections — they did — but whether those connections produced the vast and dangerous fifth column that Confederate propagandists claimed and Union prosecutors alleged.

They did not. But they produced something.

The documented cases of Copperhead cooperation with Confederate intelligence are more modest in scale and more specific in character than the sweeping conspiracy narratives suggested.

In Indiana, Confederate agents working with local Sons of Liberty contacts gathered intelligence about Union troop movements and supply arrangements that was transmitted southward through courier networks that used the existing organizational infrastructure of the secret societies. The intelligence was real, if not always timely or accurate. The organizational infrastructure was genuine, if less extensive than claimed.

In Illinois, Sons of Liberty members provided assistance to Confederate agents attempting to organize the Camp Douglas liberation plot — identifying sympathetic locals, providing safe houses, gathering information about the prison camp's security arrangements. The plot failed, as we have seen, but the assistance was real and documented in Union counterintelligence records.

In Ohio, the network around Vallandigham provided Confederate agents with a degree of political intelligence about Northern public opinion and Democratic Party dynamics that had genuine value for Confederate strategic planning — information about the strength of the peace movement, about the likelihood of Democratic electoral success, about the political conditions that might make a negotiated peace possible.

None of this added up to the vast insurrectionary conspiracy that Union prosecutors described in their indictments and Confederate agents described in their reports to Richmond. It added up to a modest intelligence and support network, rooted in genuine antiwar sentiment, penetrated from an early stage by Union counterintelligence, and capable of providing assistance but not of fundamentally altering the war's trajectory.

Colonel Henry Carrington, whose counterintelligence operation monitored the Copperhead organizations throughout 1863 and 1864, understood this better than most. His reports to Washington consistently distinguished between the genuine security concern that the organizations represented — the intelligence they provided to Confederate agents, the logistical support they offered for Confederate covert operations — and the revolutionary threat that more excitable voices in the administration insisted on seeing. Carrington took the Copperheads seriously. He did not believe they were going to overthrow the government.

He was right on both counts.

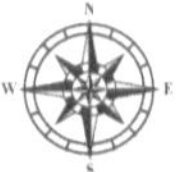

The postwar fate of the Copperhead movement was shaped largely by the war's outcome and by the political needs of the people who wrote about it.

For the Republican Party in the decades after the war, the Copperheads were useful as a symbol — proof that the Democratic Party had harbored traitors during the nation's greatest crisis, evidence that could be deployed in every election campaign for a generation. The Grand Army of the Republic, the Union veterans' organization that became one of the most powerful political forces in postwar America, waved what came to be called the "bloody shirt" — the reminder that Democrats had opposed the war — with a consistency that kept the Copperhead accusation alive long after the specific organizations had dissolved.

For the Democrats who had been Copperheads, or associated with them, or simply opposed to the war without being traitors, the postwar period required a careful navigation between acknowledging their wartime positions and defending their patriotism. Vallandigham, who had the most exposed position of anyone in this group, returned to Ohio politics and attempted to move the Democratic Party toward what he called the New Departure — abandoning the lost causes of the war years and focusing on the economic issues of the postwar era. He died in 1871 in a freak accident, accidentally shooting himself while demonstrating how a murder victim might have shot himself in a case he was defending.

The irony was not lost on anyone.

The honest assessment of the Copperhead networks and their relationship to Confederate intelligence sits somewhere between the two poles that the war's political dynamics pushed it toward.

They were not the vast and dangerous fifth column of Union prosecutor rhetoric and Confederate wishful thinking. The claimed membership figures were inflated. The revolutionary potential was essentially nonexistent. The Northwest Conspiracy failed not because Union counterintelligence was brilliant — though Carrington's operation was genuinely effective — but because the insurrectionary army that was supposed to rise was never going to rise. The men who attended Sons of Liberty meetings and paid their dues and learned the secret handshake were, most of them, antiwar voters rather than antiwar fighters. The distinction mattered enormously.

But they were not nothing. They were a genuine intelligence and support network that provided Confederate agents with assistance — modest in scale, real in fact — during a period when the Confederacy was desperately searching for any advantage it could find. They were proof that the Union home front was not monolithic, that the war was contested not just on the battlefield but in the politics and the parlors and the lodge meetings of the Northern states. They were, in their complicated, compromised, neither-quite-traitor-nor-quite-patriot way, part of the war too.

History has never quite known what to do with them. That ambivalence is, perhaps, the most honest response to people who were themselves ambivalent — who opposed a war that history has judged to have been right, for reasons that were sometimes principled and sometimes ugly and almost always more complicated than the verdicts that were handed down at the time.

They were the North's shadow — the part of the Union that wasn't quite sure it wanted to win.

OPERATIONS & ESCAPES

The Great Escape

The Libby Prison Tunnel

T he rats were the worst part.

Not the cold, though the cold in the basement of Libby Prison in the winter of 1863 was the kind that settled into your bones and stayed there. Not the darkness, though the cellar where Colonel Thomas Rose and his team were working was lit only by whatever light they could improvise from the materials available to them, which was not much. Not even the knowledge that discovery meant something considerably worse than continued imprisonment in a place that was already bad enough to have killed men through sheer accumulated misery.

The rats were everywhere. They moved through the darkness with the confidence of creatures who had established prior claim on the space and resented the human intrusion. They ran across the hands of men who were trying to dig. They investigated the faces of men who were trying to rest. They were, by multiple accounts of the men who worked in that basement, a constant and demoralizing presence in an enterprise that had no shortage of demoralizing features.

Rose and his team dug anyway. For seventeen days they dug, in shifts, in darkness, through the Virginia clay under a

Richmond street, toward a freedom that was fifty feet away and might as well have been fifty miles.

Libby Prison was not designed to be a prison.

It had been, before the war, a tobacco warehouse and ship chandlery on the corner of Twentieth and Cary Streets in Richmond — a substantial brick building of several stories, backing onto a canal that connected to the James River, situated in the industrial district of the Confederate capital with the utilitarian blankness of a building that had been built to hold goods rather than people. When the war began and the need for prisoner of war facilities rapidly outpaced the Confederacy's ability to construct them, the building was pressed into service as a holding facility for Union officers.

By 1863 it held approximately 1,200 men in conditions that the building had not been designed to sustain.

The upper floors — large open rooms that had held tobacco bales — were divided among the prisoners, who slept on the bare wood floors, cooked what food they could obtain over small fires, and organized themselves into the improvised social structures that captive populations always create when the alternative is chaos. The Confederate administration of the prison was headed by Major Thomas Turner and his subordinate, the man who became the particular object of prisoner hatred, a warehouse clerk turned prison official named Richard Turner — no relation — who was remembered by survivors as a man who brought to his work an enthusiasm that went considerably beyond the requirements of his job.

The food was inadequate. The medical care was minimal. The lice were comprehensive. Men died of disease at a rate that made the prison a slow attrition machine — not the dramatic violence of the battlefield but the grinding, unglamorous mortality of malnutrition and infection and the accumulated physical damage of a captivity that offered no prospect of improvement.

What the building also offered, though the Confederate administration did not initially appreciate this, was a basement.

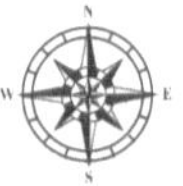

Colonel Thomas Rose was a thirty-year-old Pennsylvania infantry officer who had been captured at the Battle of Chickamauga in September 1863 and transferred to Libby Prison in the months that followed. He was not, by the accounts of the men who served with him, a particularly charismatic figure — he was methodical, quiet, persistent in the way that men who accomplish difficult things in difficult circumstances tend to be persistent, without the dramatic flair that makes for good stories but often makes for poor results.

He had been thinking about escape from the moment he arrived.

The basement of Libby Prison was theoretically off-limits to prisoners — it was a damp, dark, rat-infested space that the Confederate guards used for storage and that the prisoners had no obvious reason to access. The access point was concealed beneath a stove in one of the upper rooms — a trapdoor that Rose discovered through the kind of methodical investigation of his environment that his temperament made natural.

He went down and looked around.

What he found was a space that was miserable in almost every respect and perfect in one: it was unwatched. The Confederate guards did not regularly inspect the basement. The prisoners who knew about the trapdoor were few enough to be managed. And the basement's eastern wall, if his calculations were correct, sat beneath a vacant lot — open ground between the prison building and the street, through which a tunnel of sufficient length might provide a route to the outside.

He found twelve officers he trusted absolutely and told them what he intended to do.

The tools they had were not impressive.

A couple of case knives — the kind used for eating, with broad blades that could be used to loosen soil. A wooden box that served as a makeshift shovel for moving excavated dirt. A rope fashioned from torn clothing that allowed a man to be pulled out of the tunnel when the air inside became too thin to breathe. A small fan, improvised from material available in the prison, that one man worked continuously to push fresh air into the tunnel while another dug.

The fan operator's job was perhaps the least enviable in the operation. He sat in the basement in the dark, working the fan by hand, hour after hour, while the rats investigated him and the cold settled around him, listening for the sounds of guards above while the diggers worked ahead.

Rose organized the work in shifts — small groups rotating through the tunnel, each man digging for as long as the air would sustain him before being pulled out and replaced. The excavated soil was distributed across the basement floor and mixed with the existing dirt to avoid the accumulating pile that would have been immediately visible to anyone who inspected the space. Every trace of the tunnel's existence had to be concealed before the team emerged from the basement each morning, the trapdoor replaced and the stove moved back into position above it.

They maintained this for seventeen days.

The secrecy requirement extended not just to the Confederate guards but to the other prisoners in the building. Twelve hundred men sharing cramped quarters and desperately seeking any kind of hope or diversion represented a security risk that Rose understood clearly — a single careless word, a single prisoner who mentioned what he had heard to the wrong person, and everything was over. The team worked in silence and told nobody. In a building containing 1,200 men, they kept a secret for seventeen days.

The first attempt failed. The tunnel broke through not into the vacant lot Rose had calculated but into a small yard within the prison grounds — visible to the guards, useless as an escape route. They went back and dug a second tunnel, adjusting their calculations, working through the accumulated frustration of seventeen days of labor that had produced nothing.

The second tunnel worked.

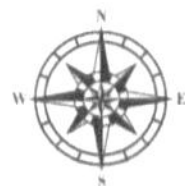

The night of February 9, 1864, was cold and clear — the kind of winter night in Richmond that made the streets relatively empty, which was what the escapees needed.

Rose went first, pulling himself through fifty feet of tunnel that was barely wide enough for a man's shoulders, emerging in the darkness of a vacant lot beside Libby Prison and lying still for a moment, listening, before moving. Behind him, one by one, came the men who had been waiting their turns in the basement — some of them officers who had known about the tunnel from the beginning, others who had been told only hours before that tonight was the night.

One hundred and nine men crawled through that tunnel over the course of the night.

The emergence point was not perfectly concealed. A Confederate sentinel was posted close enough that the escapees could hear him moving. Each man who came out of the tunnel had to wait, motionless, in the cold Virginia night, until the sentinel's back was turned before moving away into the city. It required a steadiness of nerve that not every man possessed equally, and the fact that 109 men managed it without any of them making a sound that attracted the sentinel's attention speaks to the discipline that the operation's leaders had somehow instilled in a group of men who had been waiting months for exactly this moment.

They dispersed into Richmond in the darkness — in pairs and small groups, moving through the streets of the Confederate capital in civilian clothes that some had managed to obtain and others had improvised, heading for the outskirts of the city and the Union lines beyond.

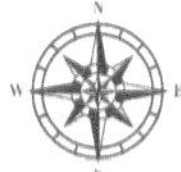

What followed was a race across Confederate Virginia that produced outcomes as varied as the men who ran it.

The lucky ones — or the prepared ones, which was often the same thing — had studied what maps they could obtain, had identified routes toward Union lines, and moved with a purposefulness that carried them through. Rose himself was recaptured within days, having been betrayed by a Black Virginian he had approached for assistance — an encounter whose precise details remain somewhat unclear in the historical record, and which Rose himself described with a restraint that left certain questions unanswered.

General Neal Dow, the oldest of the escapees at sixty years old, walked for eleven days through Confederate territory before reaching Union lines — a feat of physical endurance that impressed even the people who had organized the escape.

The final accounting, as established by postwar investigation: 59 of the 109 men who escaped reached Union lines. 48 were recaptured and returned to Libby Prison, where conditions for the returned escapees were, predictably, worse than before. 2 drowned attempting to cross the James River — the water cold enough and the current strong enough that the crossing killed men who had survived everything else the operation had required of them.

The Confederate response to the escape was immediate and comprehensive. Security at Libby Prison was drastically tightened — the basement was sealed, the guards doubled, the inspection regime intensified. Major Turner, furious at the embarrassment the escape had caused, imposed restrictions on the remaining prisoners that made the already harsh conditions harder still.

The escape also had an effect on the broader prisoner exchange negotiations that had been grinding along between the Union and Confederate governments with the intermittent progress that characterized most Civil War diplomacy. The Libby escape, and the conditions it revealed, increased

Northern public pressure for action on the prisoner exchange question — pressure that contributed, along with many other factors, to the eventual resumption of exchanges that had been suspended over the Union's refusal to include African American soldiers in the exchange system on equal terms with white soldiers.

Thomas Rose received the brevet rank of brigadier general after the war — recognition of a service that had required seventeen days of digging in the dark with a case knife, in the company of rats and cold and the constant possibility of discovery.

He had gone back into Libby after his recapture and served out the remainder of the war as a prisoner, which must have been its own particular form of torture — to have dug the tunnel, to have been the first one through it, and to have been brought back to the place you had escaped from.

He survived. He was exchanged eventually, returned to service, and was present at the war's end with the Union forces that entered Richmond in April 1865 — the city that had held him, the prison that had tried to hold him, the streets through which 109 men had walked in the February darkness of 1864, heading for the long road home.

The Railroad Raiders

Andrews' Raid and the Great Locomotive Chase

James Andrews was a difficult man to categorize, which was probably why he was so good at what he did.

He was not a soldier. He held no commission, wore no uniform, and had no official standing in the Union Army beyond the informal arrangement by which General Ormsby Mitchel used him as a spy — sending him south into Confederate territory on missions that required exactly the kind of man Andrews was: someone who could move through the Confederate world without attracting the attention that a soldier would attract, because he wasn't quite anything that the Confederate world knew how to categorize either.

He was a Kentucky civilian. He dealt in medicines and sundry goods, or said he did. He was tall, bearded, soft-spoken, and possessed of a quality that the people who knew him consistently described but struggled to name precisely — a kind of absolute surface calm that made him convincing in situations where a less controlled man would have given himself away. He had been running intelligence operations in Confederate territory since the early months of the war, moving through northern Georgia and Tennessee with a facility that suggested either exceptional skill or exceptional luck or, more likely, both.

In the spring of 1862 he came to General Mitchel with an idea.

The Western and Atlantic Railroad was the Confederate supply line that connected Atlanta to Chattanooga — the logistical spine of Confederate operations in the western theater, the track along which everything the Confederate Army in Tennessee needed moved northward. Cut it, destroy the bridges along its length, and the Confederate position in Chattanooga became untenable. The Confederate Army would have to withdraw or starve.

The plan Andrews proposed was simple in outline and extraordinarily dangerous in execution. He would take a small group of men — volunteers, in civilian clothes, posing as Kentucky civilians heading south to join the Confederate Army — infiltrate deep into Georgia, steal a locomotive, and run it north toward Chattanooga, burning the wooden bridges along the way. By the time the Confederates understood what was happening, the damage would be done.

Mitchel listened. Mitchel approved.

The twenty-two men who volunteered for the operation — Andrews plus twenty-one soldiers from Ohio infantry regiments — were not told exactly what they were volunteering for until they had already agreed to do it. This was standard practice for operations of this kind, and it raises a question that none of the surviving accounts fully resolve: if they had known the specific details in advance, how many of them would still have raised their hands?

All of them, probably. They were young, most of them — teenagers and men in their early twenties who had enlisted in the first wave of patriotic enthusiasm and who had spent the subsequent months doing the unglamorous work of army life in the western theater. An adventure was an adventure. They changed into civilian clothes, split into small groups to avoid attracting attention, and began making their way south into Confederate Georgia by whatever transportation was available.

The journey south was the operation's first test, and it nearly ended the operation before it began. A planned rendezvous point was missed. Two of the original volunteers were captured — not because they had been identified as Union operatives but through the bad luck of being in the wrong place at the wrong time, picked up in the general Confederate security sweeps that were a feature of occupied territory. They played their Kentucky civilian cover stories and survived, eventually making it back to Union lines independently, but their absence reduced Andrews's force and complicated the timeline.

The remaining twenty arrived in Marietta, Georgia, on the evening of April 11, 1862. They checked into hotels, ate dinner, slept — or tried to — and the next morning made their way separately to the Western and Atlantic Railroad station, where they boarded the northbound passenger train as ordinary travelers.

The locomotive pulling that train was called the General.

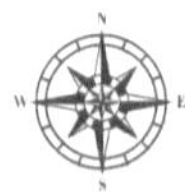

Big Shanty — now Kennesaw, Georgia — was a scheduled breakfast stop on the Western and Atlantic line, a place where the train paused for twenty minutes while passengers and crew ate at the station hotel. It was chosen as the seizure point because it had no telegraph office — meaning that once the General was taken, there was no immediate means of communicating the alarm ahead along the line.

Andrews had been watching the stop pattern for days. He knew the crew would leave the locomotive unattended. He knew the guards at Big Shanty — it was a Confederate training camp — would be eating with everyone else. He knew the window was narrow.

When the train stopped and the crew headed for the hotel, Andrews and his men moved. Some uncoupled the passenger cars from the locomotive and the three freight boxcars behind it. Others climbed into the cab. Andrews himself took the throttle.

The General moved.

A Confederate sentry saw it go and raised his musket. He didn't fire — too many civilians around, too much uncertainty about what exactly was happening. By the time the alarm was raised, the General was already accelerating northward with twenty-two men who had just committed what Confederate authorities would shortly be calling theft, sabotage, and acts of war.

The plan required speed. They needed to reach and burn the wooden bridges along the line before Confederate forces could respond, and they needed to cut the telegraph lines along the way to prevent the alarm from racing ahead of them. Andrews opened the throttle and the General ran.

What happened next was not what anyone had planned.

William Allen Fuller was the conductor of the train that Andrews's men had stolen, and he was not the kind of man who accepted the theft of his train philosophically.

He was twenty-six years old, lean and tenacious, and he started running after the General on foot the moment he understood what had happened — which was immediately, because Fuller had the particular professional pride of a railroad man and the disappearance of his locomotive in the middle of a scheduled stop was not something he needed time to process. He ran. His engineer, Jeff Cain, ran with him. A railroad foreman named Anthony Murphy ran too.

They were chasing a locomotive on foot, which was not going to work for long. But it worked long enough for Fuller to reach a handcar that had been left on the line, and the three men put the handcar on the track and began pumping northward after the General with a determination that the raiders, watching behind them, found both impressive and alarming.

Andrews had expected pursuit. He had not expected pursuit this fast, this persistent, this completely undeterred by the absurdity of chasing a locomotive on a handcar.

The raiders attempted to slow the pursuit by dropping crossties on the track behind them — logs that Fuller and his men had to stop and remove before they could continue. They cut telegraph lines at every opportunity, splicing enough wire to make rapid repair difficult. They attempted to burn the first of the wooden bridges — and here the operation's fundamental problem revealed itself.

It was raining.

The wooden bridges along the Western and Atlantic were wet from days of spring rain, and wet wood does not burn quickly. The raiders had brought no accelerants. They needed time to get a fire going — time that Fuller's pursuit was denying them at every turn. The bridges that were supposed to be burning behind them were merely scorched, still passable, still usable by the Confederate trains that Fuller was, by this point, commandeering as his handcar gave way to the locomotive Yonah and then to the faster William R. Smith and then, after a complicated piece of improvisation that involved running the Smith backward around a rival locomotive blocking the track, to the Texas — a powerful engine that Fuller was now running in reverse, full throttle, northward after the General.

The Texas was faster than the General. Fuller knew his own railroad better than the raiders did. And the General's crew was running out of fuel.

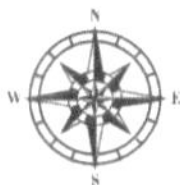

The chase covered 87 miles and lasted approximately two hours — which sounds, stated baldly, almost like a reasonable afternoon activity, and was in practice one of the more desperate experiences of the war for the men living through it.

Andrews tried everything. He dropped more crossties. He uncoupled one of the boxcars and left it on the track for the Texas to collide with — Fuller simply pushed it out of the way. He attempted again to burn a bridge, this time by setting fire to the last boxcar and uncoupling it on the bridge itself — a scheme that required the burning car to stay on the bridge long enough to set the structure alight, and which failed because Fuller pushed the burning car off the bridge before the fire could spread.

The General was out of fuel. The water in the boiler was getting dangerously low. The raiders were looking behind them at a locomotive that was getting larger in their field of vision with every passing minute, and ahead of them at a line that offered no more opportunities for the sabotage that the mission required.

Andrews stopped the General. The men scattered into the Georgia woods on both sides of the track.

All of them were captured within two weeks. The Georgia countryside was not the Virginia countryside, and the raiders' Kentucky civilian cover stories were much harder to sustain this deep into Confederate territory, where the accent and the local knowledge that made a story convincing were harder to fake.

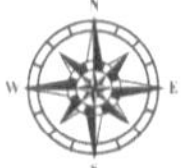

The trial that followed was swift and merciless.

Andrews and his men were not in uniform. They had entered Confederate territory under false identities, had committed acts of sabotage against Confederate infrastructure, and had done so as part of a deliberate military operation. Under the laws of war as the Confederacy interpreted them — and as most military legal authorities of the period would have agreed — they were spies and saboteurs, not prisoners of war entitled to the protections of the Geneva Convention.

Andrews was tried first, convicted of being a spy, and hanged in Atlanta on June 7, 1862. He died with the composure that had characterized everything about him — the same surface calm that had carried him through months of intelligence work in Confederate territory, present and intact at the end.

Seven of his men were hanged alongside him in subsequent executions — chosen, by an accounting that never became entirely clear, from among the captured raiders. They were soldiers who had volunteered for a mission that had not, in the end, been classified in a way that would protect them.

Eight others escaped from the Atlanta prison where they were being held — a tunnel escape that has received considerably less historical attention than the Libby Prison tunnel, perhaps because it succeeded rather than becoming the kind of dramatic story that captures historical imagination. They made it back to Union lines.

The remaining six were eventually exchanged as prisoners of war — a resolution that implicitly acknowledged their status as soldiers rather than spies, though the men who had been hanged were beyond the benefit of the acknowledgment.

The Medal of Honor had been created by Congress in December 1861 — a new decoration for a new kind of war, intended to recognize enlisted men who distinguished themselves by gallantry in action. The surviving Andrews Raiders were among the first recipients, receiving the medal in a ceremony in 1863 that recognized what they had attempted even as it could not undo what had happened to the men who had not survived to receive it.

Andrews himself received nothing — he was a civilian, and the Medal of Honor was a military decoration, and the bureaucratic categories that had contributed to his execution continued to operate after his death with the indifference of bureaucratic categories everywhere.

William Fuller — the conductor who had chased a locomotive on foot, on a handcar, and on three successive commandeered engines across 87 miles of Georgia — received recognition from the Confederate government and from the Western and Atlantic Railroad, whose property he had recovered and whose line he had kept open. He lived until 1905, long enough to attend reunions with the men who had tried to destroy the railroad he had defended, the Civil War having produced, in its later years, exactly this kind of improbable reconciliation.

The General survived the war and several subsequent decades of use on various railroads before being retired and displayed — first in Chattanooga and later in Kennesaw, Georgia, where it sits today in a museum near the spot where James Andrews stole it on a rainy April morning in 1862 and opened the throttle and ran.

The Texas, which chased it, is in Atlanta.

They are 30 miles apart. They will never close the distance.

The Woman Who Saved Washington

The Intelligence That Warned of Early's Raid

Washington in the summer of 1864 was a city that had stopped believing it could be attacked.

Three years of war had produced, in the capital, a kind of defensive complacency that is almost understandable in retrospect and was almost fatal in practice. The ring of forts that surrounded the city — built after the shock of Bull Run had demonstrated that the Confederate army was capable of things that prewar confidence had made unimaginable — had been improved and expanded until Washington was, on paper, one of the most heavily fortified cities in the world. Sixty-eight forts. Twenty miles of rifle pits. Miles of abatis — sharpened stakes and felled trees arranged to slow an attacking force. More than nine hundred artillery pieces.

What the forts lacked, in the summer of 1864, was men.

Grant had taken the Army of the Potomac south to Petersburg, where it was engaged in the grinding siege operations that would eventually end the war but that were, in July 1864, consuming the army's attention and most of its strength. The veterans who had manned Washington's defensive works had gone south with Grant. What remained were heavy artillery regiments that had been trained to serve the guns but had minimal infantry experience, convalescent soldiers recovering from wounds, and the bureaucratic and administrative apparatus of a capital city that had been at war for three years and had grown comfortable with the idea that the war was happening somewhere else.

Somewhere else was about to arrive.

Jubal Anderson Early was not, by any standard assessment, a great general. He was a capable one — aggressive, tactically competent, personally brave in the profane and irreverent mode that made him a distinctive figure in the Army of Northern Virginia even among an officer corps that had its share of characters. Robert E. Lee called him his "bad old man," which was as close to affection as Lee's reserve generally allowed, and trusted him with independent command in the Shenandoah Valley in the summer of 1864 because the strategic situation required someone who would move fast and hit hard and not stop to ask too many questions.

The strategic situation, specifically, was this: Grant's siege of Petersburg was working, slowly, in the way that sieges work — grinding down Confederate resources and manpower at a rate that the Confederacy could not sustain indefinitely. Lee needed to relieve the pressure. The most promising way to relieve it was to threaten something that Grant could not ignore — something that would force him to detach troops from Petersburg and send them north, reducing the pressure on Lee's lines.

Washington was that something.

Early crossed the Potomac into Maryland on July 6, 1864, with approximately 15,000 men — a force that was not large enough to capture and hold a properly defended Washington but was more than large enough to threaten it, to create the political crisis that a Confederate army approaching the United States capital would inevitably produce, and to potentially exploit whatever defensive gaps the city's depleted garrison presented.

The intelligence that should have provided Washington with adequate warning of Early's approach failed in almost every respect that mattered.

The failure was not a single dramatic breakdown but the accumulation of smaller failures that, in combination, produced a situation that should not have been possible — a Confederate army of 15,000 men crossing the Potomac and marching toward Washington while the Union commanders responsible for the capital's defense struggled to understand what was happening.

The cavalry screen that should have tracked Early's movements was inadequate — the Union cavalry forces in the region were too thin, too dispersed, and too poorly coordinated to maintain continuous contact with a force moving as quickly as Early was moving. Reports that reached Washington in the first days of July described Confederate activity in the Shenandoah Valley and early crossing movements but failed to convey the scale and the speed of what was underway.

The signal intelligence network — the system of observation stations and telegraph lines that connected Washington to the surrounding countryside — had gaps in exactly the places where Early's route of march would exploit them. The Maryland countryside through which Early was moving was not as thoroughly covered by Union observation posts as the Virginia theater had become, and the Confederate army was using routes that the signal officers had not prioritized.

The commander most responsible for the intelligence failure was General Lew Wallace — a general of modest military reputation who would later find considerably greater fame as the author of Ben-Hur — who commanded the Union forces in Maryland. Wallace received fragmentary and often contradictory reports about Confederate movements and attempted to assess them with the information available to him, which was insufficient. He concluded, correctly as it turned out, that something significant was moving toward Washington, but his superiors in Washington were slower to reach the same conclusion.

Secretary of War Edwin Stanton, who managed the War Department with a controlling hand that sometimes sub-stituted his judgment for that of the field commanders he was theoretically supporting, was among those who initially underestimated the threat. The telegraph traffic between Washington and Grant's headquarters at Petersburg in the first week of July 1864 has a quality of mutual reassurance that, in retrospect, reads as the communications of men who were telling each other what they wanted to hear.

Grant, pressed before Petersburg, was reluctant to believe that he needed to detach significant forces to deal with what he initially assessed as a raid rather than a serious strategic threat. Washington, reluctant to admit that it was genuinely threatened, was slow to press Grant for reinforcements with the urgency the situation required.

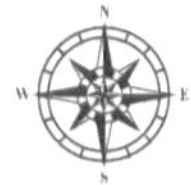

Into this intelligence vacuum came the civilians.

The woman whose story gives this chapter its title was not a trained intelligence officer. She was a Maryland farm woman — her name has been reported differently across different sources and the most thorough historical reconstructions of the Early raid acknowledge the difficulty of definitively identifying the specific individuals who carried the most significant early intelligence about his approach. What is documented, in multiple accounts, is that civilian observers in Maryland — farmers, local residents, people whose knowledge of the landscape they lived in gave them an understanding of what was moving through it that no military map could replicate — were among the first to provide accurate information about Early's strength and speed to Union authorities.

They came to Union outposts. They flagged down cavalry patrols. They sent messages through whatever channels were available to them. Some of them were women, because in the occupied and contested landscape of western Maryland in 1864, women could move more freely than men of military age, could present themselves at military posts without being immediately suspected of hostile intent, could carry intelligence that the intelligence system was not generating for itself.

The signals officer at one of the Washington area stations — his specific identity is documented in the records of the signal corps but has not been consistently preserved in the popular accounts of the raid — recorded receiving information from civilian sources in the Maryland countryside in the days before Early's arrival that was substantially more accurate about the Confederate force's size and intentions than the official military assessments being generated through normal channels.

The problem was not the information. The information was there, coming in from multiple civilian sources, painting a picture that was clear enough for anyone who was looking at the complete picture rather than the fragments.

The problem was aggregation. Nobody was pulling together the civilian reports, the cavalry observations, the signal station sightings, and the telegraph intercepts into a single coherent assessment that would have shown Washington's defenders what was actually coming toward them. The intelligence existed. The analysis did not.

Lew Wallace made his stand at the Monocacy River on July 9, 1864, with a force of approximately 6,000 men — a mixture of his own Maryland garrison troops and a division of veterans from Grant's army that had been rushed north as the scale of the threat finally registered in Washington.

He lost the battle. Early's veterans pushed through Wallace's defensive line after a day of fighting that cost both sides heavily, and Early continued his march toward Washington. But the day's delay that Monocacy imposed on Early's timetable would prove to be the margin between catastrophe and survival.

The telegraph lines were burning with traffic now — the intelligence failure of the previous week replaced by a frantic clarity about what was coming. Grant, finally persuaded that the threat was real, dispatched the Sixth Corps — veteran infantry who had been fighting in the Petersburg trenches — by ship from City Point to Washington. They arrived on July

11, disembarking at the Washington wharves and marching directly to the fort lines, their experienced presence transforming the defensive capacity of a garrison that had been genuinely incapable of sustained resistance.

Early's advance units reached Fort Stevens — on the northern edge of Washington, in what is now the Brightwood neighborhood — on July 11. They could see the Capitol dome.

What they could also see, as they assessed the fort's defenses, was that the men behind the walls had changed overnight. The convalescents and heavy artillerists who had been there the day before were still there — but among them now were Sixth Corps veterans, men who had been in the trenches before Petersburg and who knew how to fight. Early looked at what he was facing and made the calculation that most competent commanders would have made in his position.

He did not attack.

Abraham Lincoln came out to watch.

This is one of the stranger facts of the Civil War — that the President of the United States, in the middle of a Confederate attack on the capital city, went to the fort that was being fired upon and stood on the parapet to observe. He was there on July 11 and again on July 12, a tall figure in his stovepipe hat making himself a target that the Confederate sharpshooters outside the fort did not fail to notice.

The accounts of what happened next are consistent enough across multiple sources to be accepted as documented. A Union officer — the most frequently cited account identifies him as Captain Oliver Wendell Holmes Jr., the future

Supreme Court justice who was then a young officer on the staff of General Horatio Wright — reportedly shouted at the tall civilian on the parapet to get down. The civilian, who turned out to be the President, complied.

Lincoln was under fire. Actual Confederate fire, aimed at the parapet he was standing on. He was the only sitting American president to come under hostile fire while in office, a distinction he achieved through the combination of personal courage and spectacular disregard for his own safety that had characterized his relationship with the war's physical dangers throughout his time in office.

The Confederate sharpshooter who may have had Lincoln in his sights — if any of them did, which is impossible to confirm — did not fire accurately enough to matter. Lincoln came down from the parapet.

Early began his withdrawal that night, slipping back toward the Potomac in the darkness with his army intact but his mission uncompleted. Washington had held. The Sixth Corps had arrived in time. The intelligence failure of the preceding week had been salvaged, just barely, by the speed of the military response once the threat was finally understood.

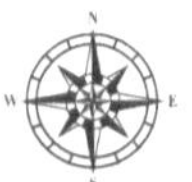

The Early raid produced a series of investigations and re-criminations that occupied Union military and political attention for weeks afterward — the natural consequence of a near-catastrophe that had been entirely preventable and that several people were therefore motivated to explain in ways that minimized their own contribution to the failure.

The intelligence lessons were eventually absorbed, though not as quickly or as completely as the near-miss warranted. The gaps in the Maryland signal observation network were addressed. The cavalry screening arrangements for the approaches to Washington were improved. The aggregation problem — the failure to combine multiple intelligence streams into a coherent assessment — received attention from officers who had watched the Early raid demonstrate its consequences in the most direct possible way.

The civilian sources who had provided the most accurate early intelligence about Early's approach received no formal recognition. They were not part of the military intelligence system. Their contributions were noted in some unit records and forgotten in others. The Maryland farm woman — or women — who had carried information about Confederate movements to Union posts in the first days of July 1864, who had done what the cavalry screen and the signal network had failed to do, were absorbed back into the landscape they had come from.

The history of the Early raid remembers the battle at Monocacy and Lincoln on the parapet at Fort Stevens. It remembers Early's decision not to attack and the Sixth Corps arriving in the nick of time.

It does not usually remember the civilians who were sounding the alarm before anyone with a uniform was listening.

They were there. They were right. They were not enough, quite, to close the gap that the intelligence failure had opened — but they were what stood between that failure and something worse.

In the secret war, that was sometimes the best that could be said of anyone.

The Spy Who Came in From the Cold

Double Agents and Turned Operatives

The intelligence business runs on betrayal.

This is not a cynical observation. It is a structural one. Every spy is, by definition, betraying something — an employer, a country, a cause, the people who trust them. Every double agent is betraying two things simultaneously, which requires a particular kind of psychological architecture that most people don't possess and that the ones who do possess it carry at considerable cost. The turned operative — the agent who switches sides under pressure, who trades what they know for what they need — is betraying everyone at once, and knows it, and does it anyway because the alternative is worse.

The Civil War produced all of these types in abundance. It was, in certain respects, the ideal war for betrayal — a conflict fought between people who shared a language, a culture, and in many cases a family, in which the lines between the sides were permeable in ways that the wars of the twentieth century would make impossible. A man who looked Confederate could be Union. A woman who sounded

Southern could be Northern. The social signals that served as identity markers in peacetime became, in wartime, the tools of deception.

Some people were very good at this. Some were not good enough. The difference, in most cases, was the difference between living and dying.

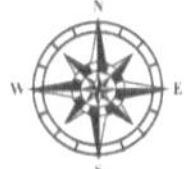

Timothy Webster was Allan Pinkerton's best agent, which meant he was probably the best Union intelligence operative operating in Confederate territory during the first two years of the war.

He was English-born, forty years old when the war began, a former New York City police officer who had been working for the Pinkerton agency since the 1850s. He was not physically remarkable — medium height, ordinary features, the kind of face that didn't attract attention in a crowd. This was an asset. The agents who got caught, in Pinkerton's experience, were often the ones whose appearance was memorable. Webster was forgettable in exactly the right ways.

His cover was a Confederate sympathizer from Baltimore — a man whose Southern sympathies had driven him from his home after Union occupation made life there uncomfortable, who had connections in Richmond society and was willing to use them in service of the cause. He built the cover with the thoroughness that Pinkerton demanded and the instinct for human psychology that made him exceptional. He attended the right social gatherings. He said the right things. He cultivated relationships with Confederate officials and military officers who found him charming and trustworthy and never quite understood why.

The intelligence he sent back to Pinkerton was remarkable. Confederate troop dispositions. The state of Confederate morale. Details of Confederate military planning that Pinkerton passed to McClellan and that influenced Union operational decisions during the early months of the war. Webster moved through Richmond society with a freedom that reflected both his skill and the Confederate intelligence establishment's failure to adequately screen the sympathizers who were moving freely through their capital.

He made multiple round trips between Richmond and the North — carrying dispatches in both directions, maintaining his cover in Richmond while reporting to Pinkerton in the North, living the double life that intelligence work requires with an apparent ease that concealed whatever it actually cost him. The cost was real. Living in constant performance, maintaining a false identity under conditions where discovery meant death, sustaining the social relationships that were the cover's infrastructure while simultaneously working to undermine the people those relationships connected him to — this was not a sustainable psychological state, and Webster's health deteriorated under the strain in ways that would eventually contribute to his capture.

By the winter of 1862 he was ill — seriously enough that he was bedridden in his Richmond lodgings, unable to make his scheduled contact with Pinkerton's network. The silence from Richmond alarmed Pinkerton, who made the decision that ended Webster's career and his life: he sent two agents to Richmond to find out what had happened.

The two agents Pinkerton sent — John Scully and Pryce Lewis — were themselves experienced operatives. They were also, as it turned out, known to Confederate counterintelligence from a previous operation in which they had been arrested and released. When they arrived in Richmond and began making inquiries about Webster, Confederate authorities arrested them.

Under pressure — the nature and degree of which neither man described in detail in subsequent accounts, for reasons that are not difficult to understand — Scully and Lewis identified Webster as a Union agent.

The betrayal was not a simple calculation. They were facing execution themselves. They had information that could save their lives. Whether what they did constitutes treachery or survival depends on moral frameworks that are easier to apply from a distance than from inside a Richmond jail cell facing the prospect of hanging.

Webster was arrested in his sickbed. He was tried by a Confederate military commission, convicted of espionage, and sentenced to death. He petitioned for clemency on the grounds that he was too ill to be hanged — a petition that the Confederate authorities denied with a thoroughness that suggested they were determined to make an example. He was carried to the gallows on a chair.

The hanging itself went wrong. The rope broke on the first attempt, dropping Webster to the ground alive. He had to be helped back to his feet, re-secured, and hanged again. He died on the second attempt. He was the first spy executed in the Civil War, and the manner of his death was reported in Northern newspapers with the outrage that any execution of a spy produces in the country that sent him.

Scully and Lewis were eventually exchanged. They returned to the North and to lives that continued past the war. Webster's life ended in a Richmond jail yard on April 29, 1862. He was forty-one years old.

Pinkerton never fully forgave himself for sending the agents whose identification of Webster had led to his execution. He described the decision in his postwar memoir with a restraint that suggested the wound was still present. He had sent men to find his best agent and had caused his death. That is the kind of accounting that does not resolve cleanly, regardless of how many years pass.

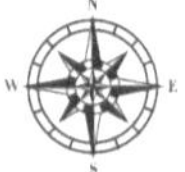

Sam Davis was twenty-one years old and he was not going to tell them anything.

This was clear to the Union officers who interrogated him almost from the beginning — clear in the way that certain things become clear when you are looking at someone whose decision has already been made and whose demeanor communicates that fact without ambiguity. Davis was a Confederate scout from Tennessee, captured behind Union lines in November 1863 near Pulaski with detailed intelligence about Union troop dispositions — maps, reports, information that was current and accurate and that could only have come from a source with significant access to Union military information.

The source was the question. Who had given Davis this intelligence? Where was the penetration in the Union military establishment that was producing reports of this quality?

General Grenville Dodge, the Union commander responsible for military intelligence in the western theater and one of the more capable intelligence officers the Union produced, understood immediately that the intelligence Davis was carrying represented a serious breach. He also understood, from his first interrogation of Davis, that getting the young

Tennessean to identify his source was going to require either extraordinary persuasion or extraordinary pressure.

He tried both. He offered Davis his life and his freedom in exchange for the name of his source. Davis declined. He told Davis, with the directness of a man who meant what he said, that the alternative to cooperation was execution. Davis said he understood.

The source, it is now generally believed, was a Confederate agent named E. Coleman who had penetrated Dodge's own intelligence network — a mole operating inside the Union intelligence establishment whose exposure would have been a significant counterintelligence success. Davis knew who Coleman was. He knew what Coleman's exposure would mean for the Confederate intelligence operation in the western theater.

He didn't tell them.

He was hanged on November 27, 1863, in Pulaski, Tennessee — the town where, two years later, the Ku Klux Klan would be founded by Confederate veterans. He asked to be allowed to pray before the execution. He was. He said, by the accounts of the Union soldiers present, that he could die for his country but he could not betray it.

He was twenty-one years old.

The Confederate Army made Sam Davis a hero — a martyr of the kind that lost causes require, someone whose courage in the face of death can be held up as evidence that the cause deserved the devotion it inspired. Tennessee erected a statue of him. The Sam Davis Home in Smyrna, Tennessee, became a heritage site. His youth and his refusal and the manner of his death made him, in Confederate memory, something close to a saint.

The historical reality is more straightforward and no less moving for being stripped of its commemorative additions. He was a young man who had made a commitment and kept it under the worst possible pressure. Whatever the cause he was serving — and the cause of the Confederacy was not a cause that history has judged well — the personal courage that keeping that commitment required was real and absolute.

The turned agents — the ones who went the other way, who took the offer that Davis refused — are harder to write about, because they survived.

Survival in this context creates its own complications. The turned agent who provides his former employers' intelligence service with information about their networks and operations is simultaneously a valuable asset and an unreliable witness — motivated to please his new handlers, aware that the value of what he provides is the measure of his continued safety, equipped with strong incentives to tell his handlers what they want to hear rather than what is actually true.

Union counterintelligence developed, over the course of the war, a sophisticated enough understanding of this problem to handle turned Confederate agents with appropriate skepticism — using the information they provided as one input among several rather than as a reliable standalone source, cross-referencing their reports against other intelligence, testing their reliability through assignments whose results could be independently verified.

The cases that are most thoroughly documented in Union military records involve Confederate agents who were captured while conducting operations in the North — courier networks, sabotage operatives, the various figures who passed through the Canadian operations and the Copperhead networks — and who were offered the choice that the Union counterintelligence system regularly presented to captured enemy operatives: provide information about Confederate networks and personnel in exchange for their freedom, or face prosecution as spies.

Many of them took the offer. The intelligence they provided was of varying quality and verified reliability. Some of it was genuinely useful — identifying Confederate agents who were subsequently apprehended, mapping organizational structures that Union counterintelligence had been unable to penetrate through other means. Some of it was self-serving fabrication, designed to appear cooperative while protecting the assets the turned agent most wanted to protect.

Distinguishing between the two categories required exactly the kind of analytical skepticism that the best Union counterintelligence officers brought to the problem, and that the worst ones consistently failed to apply.

The moral landscape of Civil War intelligence work resists the clean categories that war narrative prefers.

Timothy Webster was a hero of the Union cause whose skill and courage produced intelligence of genuine value — and whose story ends with him being carried to a gallows on a chair because two frightened men told the truth about him under circumstances that made truth-telling the only way to survive. Was what Scully and Lewis did a betrayal? Survival?

Both? The answer changes depending on where you stand and what you're willing to count as mitigating circumstance.

Sam Davis was a twenty-one-year-old who died for a cause that was fighting to preserve human slavery — and who demonstrated, in the manner of his death, a personal courage that makes any simple moral verdict feel inadequate. He was brave. His cause was wrong. Both of these things are true simultaneously, and the tension between them is not resolvable by choosing one over the other.

The turned agents who took the offer of freedom in exchange for information were neither heroes nor villains — they were people making the best calculation available to them in circumstances that offered no good options. Some of them were telling the truth. Some were not. The handlers who used their information knew this and worked accordingly, which is exactly what intelligence work requires.

The spy who comes in from the cold — John le Carré's phrase, borrowed here because it captures something true about what it feels like to cross from one side to the other in conditions of extreme cold and extreme danger — does not come in clean. Nobody in this business comes in clean. They come in with whatever they have left after the experience of living in two worlds simultaneously, of being trusted by people they were deceiving, of knowing that discovery meant the kind of ending that Timothy Webster met in a Richmond jail yard on a spring morning in 1862.

Some of them made it. Some of them didn't. All of them paid something that doesn't appear in any official accounting of the war's costs — the interior price of a life lived under cover, where the face you show the world is not your face and the name you answer to is not your name and the only truth you possess is the one you're paid to conceal.

That price was real. It was paid in full.

The Telegraph War

Wiretapping and Electronic Intelligence in the Civil War

T he wire hummed with other people's secrets.

This was the fundamental discovery of the Civil War's intelligence services — that the telegraph, which had transformed military communication by allowing messages to travel at the speed of electricity rather than the speed of a horse, had also created a vulnerability that no previous communication system had possessed in quite this form. A message carried by a courier could be intercepted only if the courier was intercepted. A message traveling along a wire could be intercepted anywhere along the wire's length by anyone with the equipment and the knowledge to do it — and the equipment was not complicated and the knowledge was not rare.

Tap the wire. Listen. Read what the enemy was saying to itself before it finished saying it.

Both sides understood this from early in the war. Both sides did it when they could. The results, in specific documented cases, shaped the outcome of specific battles and operations in ways that the official histories of those battles often failed to acknowledge — because the intelligence that shaped them was classified, or because the commanders who benefited from it were reluctant to reveal how they had obtained it, or simply because the history of what moved along the wires was harder to reconstruct than the history of what happened on the ground.

The telegraph war ran alongside the shooting war for four years. It was quieter, more invisible, and in certain moments more consequential than anything happening on the battlefield.

The Union Military Telegraph system was one of the genuine organizational achievements of the Civil War — a communication network built from essentially nothing in the first months of the war and expanded, over four years, into the most extensive military communications infrastructure the world had ever seen.

At its peak it comprised over 15,000 miles of wire, connecting Union headquarters, field commands, supply depots, and the War Department in Washington in a network that transmitted more than six million messages over the course of the war. The men who operated it — the military telegraph operators who worked the keys in tents and converted buildings and improvised stations across every theater of the war — were among the most valuable and least celebrated people in the Union Army. They were not soldiers in the conventional sense. They did not carry weapons into battle. They sat at tables and worked their instruments and processed the traffic of a war that could not have been managed without them.

The construction of the network was itself a military operation. Telegraph construction crews followed the Union armies in the field — stringing wire along roads and across rivers, connecting newly captured territory to the existing network, repairing lines that Confederate cavalry raids cut and that the construction crews repaired with a speed that frustrated Confederate commanders who calculated their raids in terms of communication disruption and found the disruption lasting hours rather than the days they had hoped for.

The War Department telegraph office in Washington — the room where Lincoln spent his hours reading the traffic, where Charles Tinker and his colleagues worked the cipher systems — was the hub of a network that had no precedent in military history. Before the telegraph, a commanding general communicated with his subordinates at the speed of horseback. During the Civil War, Grant sitting at City Point could exchange messages with Sherman in Georgia, Sheridan in the Shenandoah Valley, and the War Department in Washington within the space of an afternoon.

This was new. It changed everything about how war was commanded and controlled. It also created, everywhere along its 15,000 miles of wire, opportunities for anyone who wanted to listen.

Tapping a telegraph line required, in the Civil War era, a simple set of tools and a working knowledge of Morse code.

The physical connection was made by attaching a small induction coil — a device that could be clamped to the telegraph wire without cutting it — and connecting it to a receiving instrument. The induction coil picked up the electrical signals passing through the wire without interrupting them, allowing the interceptor to read the traffic without the sender or receiver knowing the line had been tapped. It was, in the terminology of the twentieth century, a passive intercept — leaving no trace, producing no interruption, invisible to everyone except the person reading the traffic.

Confederate cavalry commanders understood the value of this capability early and exploited it with varying degrees of sophistication. The raids that Confederate cavalry conducted behind Union lines were not purely military operations — they were intelligence operations as well, and the telegraph lines that ran through the Union rear areas were as much a target as the supply depots and rail lines that attracted more obvious attention.

The specific documented cases where tapped Union telegraph traffic produced genuine operational intelligence for Confederate commanders are scattered through the historical record — appearing in Union after-action reports that noted message security failures, in Confederate commanders' memoirs that described intelligence coups, and in the investigations that Union counterintelligence conducted when it became clear that specific operations had been compromised by telegraph interception.

One of the most consequential documented cases involved Confederate General Nathan Bedford Forrest's operations in Tennessee — where tapped Union telegraph lines provided Confederate intelligence with advance warning of Union cavalry movements that allowed Forrest's smaller force to position itself advantageously in engagements where its numerical disadvantage should have been decisive. The specific details of the interception are documented in Union military records that postdate the engagements and were generated by the investigations that followed.

But the most spectacular practitioner of the telegraph war on the Confederate side was not Forrest. It was a twenty-two-year-old Kentucky civilian who signed his messages with a single word.

Lightning.

George Ellsworth had learned telegraphy as a teenager and had achieved, by the time the war began, the level of proficiency that the telegraph industry called a first-class operator — someone who could send and receive at speeds that lesser operators found difficult to follow, whose fist on the key was distinctive and recognizable to other operators the way a voice is recognizable, whose ear for the rhythm of incoming Morse could distinguish between operators and identify specific individuals by their sending style.

John Hunt Morgan recognized what he had when Ellsworth came to him in 1862, and he used it.

Morgan's cavalry raids through Kentucky and Tennessee were among the more spectacular Confederate operations of the war's middle period — fast-moving, destructive, embarrassing to Union commanders who found their supply lines and their communication networks disrupted by a force that seemed to appear and disappear at will. Ellsworth was the intelligence dimension of those raids — riding with the column, tapping Union lines whenever the opportunity presented itself, reading Union traffic in real time and feeding the intelligence directly to Morgan.

What Ellsworth did with the lines he tapped went beyond passive interception. He sent messages.

The practice of sending false messages on compromised telegraph lines — inserting fabricated traffic into the Union communication system to confuse commanders and misdirect pursuit — was Ellsworth's particular contribution to Civil War intelligence technique, and he was extraordinarily good at it. He could imitate the sending style of specific Union operators — having listened to them long enough to learn their individual rhythms — and send messages in their names that were indistinguishable, to the receiving end, from the genuine article.

During Morgan's Christmas Raid of December 1862, Ellsworth tapped into the Union telegraph network and conducted an operation that became one of the more celebrated episodes in the history of Civil War intelligence. He intercepted Union messages about the pursuit of Morgan's column, used that intelligence to guide Morgan's route, and then — in the part of the story that has been told and retold precisely because it captures something essential about Ellsworth's character — had an extended conversation with Union telegraph operators along the line while Morgan's men were simultaneously destroying the line at the points the conversation was crossing.

The Union operators, believing they were communicating with a colleague, provided information about Union troop dispositions and pursuit plans. Ellsworth thanked them, wished them well, and signed off. By the time Union commanders understood what had happened, Morgan's column was miles away and the telegraph line was down.

The specific content of the messages Ellsworth sent and received during the Christmas Raid is documented in Union military records and in postwar accounts by participants on both sides — sources that are consistent enough in their broad outlines to be accepted as substantially accurate while acknowledging that the dramatic details of specific conversations were inevitably shaped by the storytelling impulses of the people who recorded them.

The Union counterintelligence response to Confederate telegraph tapping evolved over the course of the war from reactive to systematic — moving from the discovery of specific compromises and the patching of specific vulnerabilities to the development of organizational practices and technical measures that reduced the threat across the entire network.

The cipher systems that Anson Stager had developed provided the primary defense — a message encrypted in the route cipher was useless to an interceptor who couldn't read it, and the Confederate intelligence services never developed the capability to break the Union cipher with the consistency that would have made widespread telegraph interception a reliable intelligence source. Ellsworth could read Union traffic in plain language when Union operators were careless enough to send it that way, but the War Department traffic — the messages that mattered most strategically — moved in cipher that he couldn't crack.

Authentication protocols were developed to address the false-message problem that Ellsworth's operations had demonstrated. Specific code words and authentication phrases were introduced that authorized operators were required to include in their messages — verification elements that an outsider like Ellsworth, however good his ear for sending styles, would not know. The protocols were not perfectly implemented or perfectly maintained, but they reduced the vulnerability significantly.

The deliberate use of compromised lines to transmit false information was perhaps the most sophisticated counterintelligence measure the Union employed — and the one that most directly mirrored what Ellsworth had been doing to the

Union. When Union counterintelligence identified a line as compromised — or suspected it might be — it sometimes used the line to transmit false intelligence designed to be intercepted and acted upon by Confederate commanders. The practice required careful management, because the false messages had to be convincing enough to be believed without being specific enough to cause genuine harm if Confederate commanders acted on them in ways that could not be anticipated.

The documented cases of deliberate Union false-message operations are fewer than the cases of Confederate tapping, partly because the Union practice left a different kind of paper trail — the planning of a disinformation operation tends to be less well documented than the receipt of intelligence that turns out to have been fabricated. But the practice existed, and the officers responsible for it understood, in embryo, the principles that would govern signals intelligence and electronic deception in the conflicts of the following century.

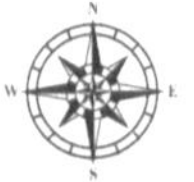

George Ellsworth survived the war. He outlasted Morgan — who was killed in September 1864 in a Union cavalry raid on his headquarters in Greeneville, Tennessee, shot in the garden of a house where he was sleeping — and he outlasted the Confederate cause he had served with such ingenuity.

He returned to civilian telegraphy after the war, working the lines of the expanding commercial telegraph network in the decades that followed, one of thousands of skilled operators whose wartime experiences became, in peacetime, simply the backstory of an ordinary professional life. He gave occasional interviews about his wartime adventures to journalists who found the Lightning stories irresistible — the young man who had talked to Union operators while his comrades cut their wires, who had impersonated enemy colleagues and misdirected enemy pursuit and read enemy secrets from a clamp attached to a copper wire in the Virginia countryside.

The stories were good. They were also true, which made them better.

The telegraph war he had helped to shape had no clean ending — it simply became, as the shooting war ended and the armies went home, a set of techniques and vulnerabilities and counterintelligence responses that the next generation of military communicators would inherit and refine and eventually transform, through the technologies that followed, into something that Ellsworth would not have recognized as descended from his clamp and his key and his extraordinary ear for the sounds of other people's secrets moving along a wire.

But descended it was. The wire hummed with secrets in 1862. The fiber optic cables hum with them still.

The fundamentals have not changed. Only the speed.

The Secret War at Sea

Confederate Naval Intelligence and the Commerce Raiders

The Alabama was built in a British shipyard and everyone knew it.

That was the problem — or rather, that was one of the problems, nested inside a larger problem that the Union government spent three years trying to solve and the Confederate government spent the same three years trying to prevent it from solving. The larger problem was this: the Confederacy had no navy worth the name and needed one, Britain had shipyards capable of building one and a commercial interest in doing so, and the neutrality laws that were supposed to prevent a neutral country from supplying warships to a belligerent were written with enough ambiguity that a sufficiently creative interpretation could drive a fully-armed commerce raider through them.

James Dunwody Bulloch was the man who found the interpretation and drove the ships through it.

He was a Georgian by birth, a career naval officer who had resigned his United States Navy commission when the war began and reported to Confederate Secretary of the Navy Stephen Mallory with a proposition: send him to England, give him money and authority, and he would build the Confederate Navy in British shipyards while the British government looked the other way. Mallory sent him. What Bulloch accomplished in Liverpool over the next three years was one of the more remarkable procurement and intelligence operations of the entire war — not just the construction and deployment of the commerce raiders that devastated Union maritime commerce, but the intelligence network that made those raiders effective once they were at sea.

The commerce raiding campaign that Confederate cruisers conducted against Union merchant shipping was, by any measure, one of the most strategically effective Confederate operations of the war.

The numbers are striking. The CSS Alabama alone, over a career of two years and roughly 75,000 miles of ocean, captured or destroyed 65 Union merchant vessels before being sunk by the USS Kearsarge off Cherbourg, France, in June 1864. The CSS Florida captured or destroyed 37 vessels. The CSS Shenandoah, which continued operating after the war had ended because its commander did not receive reliable news of the Confederate surrender until August 1865, captured or destroyed 38 vessels — including a significant portion of the American whaling fleet in the Pacific.

The total damage to Union maritime commerce was enormous. Marine insurance rates on American vessels rose so dramatically that many Union shippers transferred their cargoes to neutral — primarily British — vessels to avoid the Confederate raider threat. The American merchant marine, which had been one of the largest in the world before the war, was devastated — a damage so severe that American commercial shipping never fully recovered its prewar position.

None of this happened by accident. It happened because the Confederate commerce raiders had information — about where Union merchant vessels were, where they were going, what they were carrying, and which routes offered the most productive hunting grounds. That information came from a network of agents and contacts that Bulloch and his colleagues had developed across the Atlantic world, in the neutral ports where Union and Confederate interests intersected and where money and Southern sympathy could purchase the intelligence that a raider needed to find its targets.

Liverpool was the center of the Confederate naval intelligence operation in Europe, and James Bulloch was its architect.

He arrived in Liverpool in June 1861 with a mandate, a budget, and the particular advantage of a man who knew the maritime world from the inside — who understood how ships were built and armed and deployed, who had contacts in the British shipping and shipbuilding industry from his prewar naval career, and who could navigate the commercial and legal landscape of the Liverpool waterfront with the confidence of someone who had been there before.

His primary task was procurement — the construction of Confederate warships in British yards under contracts that were structured to avoid, or at least to make arguable, the provisions of the British Foreign Enlistment Act that prohibited the construction of warships for belligerents. The legal strategy he developed was elegant: the ships would be built without their armaments, sold to nominally neutral purchasers, taken to a rendezvous point outside British territorial waters, and there transferred to Confederate crews and armed with weapons that had been shipped separately on another vessel.

The Alabama was built under this arrangement as Hull Number 290 at the Laird Brothers shipyard in Birkenhead, just across the Mersey from Liverpool. Her construction was an open secret in Liverpool maritime circles — everyone in the shipping world knew what she was and who she was for, and the British government's enforcement of its neutrality laws was, during the Alabama's construction, sufficiently relaxed to allow the ship to be completed and launched before legal proceedings against her could succeed.

The intelligence dimension of Bulloch's Liverpool operation extended beyond ship procurement. He maintained a network of contacts — agents, Confederate sympathizers, commercial contacts with access to information about Union shipping — who provided the Confederate Navy Department with intelligence about Union naval movements, the deployment of Union warships hunting Confederate raiders, and the commercial intelligence about merchant ship schedules and routes that the raider commanders needed to find their targets.

The network of Confederate agents in neutral Atlantic ports was the operational intelligence infrastructure that made the commerce raiding campaign work day-to-day.

Bermuda and Nassau were the primary Confederate trans-shipment points in the western Atlantic — neutral British colonial ports through which the supplies and materials that the Confederate blockade runners needed moved in both directions. They were also intelligence collection points, where Confederate agents monitored Union naval deployments, gathered information about the movements of Union merchant vessels, and passed that information to Confederate raider commanders through whatever communication channels were available.

The intelligence that the Alabama's captain, Raphael Semmes, received about Union shipping came from multiple sources — the Confederate agent network in Atlantic ports, the British commercial press that published shipping intelligence openly, the information that Semmes gathered directly from the vessels he captured and their crews, and the broader maritime intelligence that circulated among the Confederate sympathizers in the British and European shipping communities who found it natural to share information with Confederate officers they met in port.

Semmes was himself a sophisticated intelligence consumer. He understood that the effectiveness of his raiding campaign depended on being where the Union merchant traffic was, which required knowing where that traffic was going. He read the captured manifests and logs of the vessels he took with the attention of someone extracting operational intelligence — understanding that what one ship's papers told him about trade routes and port schedules applied to the dozens of other vessels making the same voyages.

In Havana, Confederate agents with access to the Cuban shipping community gathered intelligence about Union vessels moving through the Caribbean. In the Azores, Confederate sympathizers in the Portuguese-American community provided Semmes with information that allowed him to position the Alabama at rendezvous points where Union whalers were known to operate. In Cape Town, Confederate agents reported on Union naval vessels using the port and on the commercial traffic that offered potential targets in the South Atlantic and Indian Ocean.

The network was informal by the standards of organized intelligence services — it relied on personal relationships, shared sympathies, and commercial connections rather than on a structured system of reporting and analysis. But it was real, and it was effective, and it produced the operational intelligence that allowed Confederate raiders to find Union vessels in hundreds of thousands of square miles of open ocean.

The Union counterintelligence response to Bulloch's Liverpool operation was conducted primarily by two men whose efforts, combined, eventually succeeded in shutting down the Confederate naval procurement network in Britain — though not before the most damaging raiders had already been launched.

Henry Sanford was the United States Minister to Belgium but effectively served as the senior Union intelligence officer in Europe — running a network of agents and informers across the continent who monitored Confederate procurement activities and reported to Secretary of State Seward in Washington. His operation was better funded than Bulloch's but less tightly managed, and its effectiveness was inconsistent.

Thomas Dudley was the United States Consul in Liverpool, and he was the man who came closest to being Bulloch's direct adversary — a New Jersey lawyer who arrived in Liverpool in late 1861 and immediately began building a network of informers and contacts in the Liverpool maritime community to monitor Confederate shipbuilding activities and gather the evidence that would allow the British government to be pressured into enforcing its neutrality laws.

Dudley understood that the legal strategy required evidence — specific, documented, legally admissible evidence that the ships being built in British yards were intended for Confederate military use rather than for the nominally neutral commercial purposes that the builders claimed. He paid informers inside the Laird Brothers shipyard. He hired private investigators to monitor the movements of Confederate agents and the progress of ship construction. He gathered affidavits from dockworkers and maritime professionals who had direct knowledge of the ships' intended purposes.

The evidence he gathered about the Alabama was compelling enough that Union Ambassador Charles Adams presented it to the British Foreign Office with an urgency that should have been sufficient to prevent the ship's departure. The British government's response was delayed — whether through bureaucratic inefficiency, deliberate foot-dragging, or the influence of the powerful commercial interests that wanted the Laird Brothers' contracts to proceed — long enough for the Alabama to escape into international waters before any order to detain her could be served.

It was one of the most consequential diplomatic failures of the Civil War, and the British government would eventually acknowledge as much — paying the United States fifteen and a half million dollars in the Alabama Claims settlement of 1872, compensation for the damage that a ship built in a British yard and enabled by British inaction had inflicted on American commerce.

Bulloch's subsequent procurement efforts — the construction of the CSS Georgia, the CSS Rappahannock, and most ambitiously the construction of two ironclad rams intended for direct naval action against the Union blockade fleet — ran into increasingly effective resistance from Dudley's counter-intelligence operation and the diplomatic pressure that the Alabama's depredations had generated in Washington.

The ironclad rams were the closest the Confederacy came to a genuine naval breakthrough in European waters. Two powerful warships, built by Laird Brothers and capable of breaking the Union blockade, were under construction in Birkenhead by 1863 — far more dangerous to the Union war effort than any commerce raider, because their target was not merchant shipping but the Union Navy itself.

Dudley documented their construction with the same thoroughness he had applied to the Alabama. Adams presented the evidence to the British Foreign Office with an explicitness that moved beyond diplomatic language — his note of September 5, 1863, warning that the departure of the rams would be "superfluous" to add would be "a matter of serious moment" has been summarized in the historical memory as "it would be superfluous in me to point out to your Lordship that this is war." The British government, finally persuaded that the diplomatic and legal risk of allowing the rams to depart outweighed the commercial benefits of the Laird Brothers' contracts, seized the vessels.

It was the effective end of Bulloch's procurement program. The Confederate Navy would receive no more warships from British yards. The commerce raiders already at sea would continue operating until they were sunk or the war ended — the Shenandoah pursuing Union whalers in the Pacific until August 1865, months after the Confederate government had ceased to exist — but the pipeline that had produced them was closed.

James Bulloch never returned to the United States after the war. He remained in Liverpool, where he had built his operation and where he had made his life during the war years, working in the maritime commerce that had been his professional world before the conflict had redirected his energies. He wrote his memoirs — *The Secret Service of the Confederate States in Europe* — a remarkably detailed and honest account of his wartime activities that remains one of the primary sources for the history of Confederate naval intelligence in Europe.

He was, by his nephew's later account, a reserved man who did not discuss his wartime service in casual conversation. The nephew was Theodore Roosevelt, who credited his uncle as an important early influence and who dedicated his own naval history, *The Naval War of 1812*, in part to Bulloch.

The CSS Alabama rests on the bottom of the English Channel, about six miles off Cherbourg, where the Kearsarge put her in June 1864. The wreck was located in 1984 and has been partially excavated — artifacts recovered from the site are now held in French and American museums. Raphael Semmes survived the sinking, was rescued by a British yacht, and eventually made his way back to the Confederacy, where he was given command of the James River Squadron and promoted to rear admiral.

He lived until 1877. He never expressed regret about the Alabama's career or the damage it had done. He believed, with the conviction of a man who had spent two years at sea in service of a cause he considered just, that what he had done was what the war required.

The Union merchants whose ships he had burned might have seen it differently. Seeing it differently, in the aftermath of a war, is what survivors get to do.

The Alabama is past all that now — past argument, past justification, past the loyalties that sent her to sea and the loyalties that sank her. She is a shipwreck on the floor of the English Channel, holding whatever she holds, keeping whatever secrets remain.

The water above her moves. The ships pass over.

The Assassination Conspiracy

Intelligence Failures and the Death of Lincoln

T he war was over.

That, in the end, may have been the most significant contributing factor to what happened at Ford's Theatre on the night of April 14, 1865 — not the specific intelligence failures, not the inadequate security arrangements, not the particular vulnerabilities of a theatre building with multiple entrances and a state box accessible from a public corridor. Those things mattered, and they will be examined here with the care they deserve. But underneath all of them was a more fundamental failure: the psychological failure of a city and a government and a security apparatus that had spent four years at maximum alert and had, in the first weeks of April 1865, begun to exhale.

Lee had surrendered at Appomattox on April 9. The war, to all practical purposes, was done. Washington was celebrating — the kind of sustained, disbelieving, exhausted celebration of people who have been living inside a catastrophe for so long that its ending feels unreal. Illuminations lit the public buildings. Crowds moved through the streets. The tension that had governed the city's emotional life since the first shots at Fort Sumter was releasing, slowly, in the way that four years of tension releases — not all at once but in stages, each day slightly less vigilant than the day before.

John Wilkes Booth had not surrendered. His war was not over.

The threat to Abraham Lincoln's life had been real and documented from the moment his election made him a target.

The Baltimore Plot of February 1861 — the conspiracy that Pinkerton's operatives had uncovered and that had resulted in Lincoln's midnight passage through the city — was the first serious documented assassination threat against a president-elect in American history. Lincoln had survived it, been mocked for the manner of his survival, and continued into a presidency in which the threats did not diminish and the security arrangements remained, by any reasonable assessment, inadequate.

The security apparatus available to protect the President of the United States in 1865 was, by modern standards, almost unimaginably thin. There was no Secret Service — that organization would not be created until after the assassination, in July 1865, though the legislation authorizing it had been drafted before Lincoln's death and was focused on currency counterfeiting rather than executive protection. Lincoln's personal security consisted of a rotating detail of four Washington Metropolitan Police officers who took turns accompanying him, a small military guard at the White House, and whatever informal protection was provided by the personal bodyguards and aides who traveled with him.

Ward Hill Lamon, Lincoln's old Illinois friend who had accompanied him on the midnight Baltimore journey and who took his protective responsibilities with unusual seriousness, had begged Lincoln repeatedly to exercise more caution about public appearances and to accept better security arrangements. Lincoln was a poor subject for this kind of advice. He disliked the formality of heavy security, found it inconsistent with his democratic instincts, and had reached a philosophical accommodation with the possibility of his own assassination that made his security advisors' arguments difficult to sustain.

He had told various people, at various times, that if someone was determined to kill him, security arrangements would not prevent it — that a man willing to give his own life could always find a way to take the president's. This was not an unreasonable assessment of the fundamental mathematics of executive protection. It was also the kind of thinking that made Lincoln a difficult person to keep alive.

Lamon was not at Ford's Theatre on the night of April 14. He was in Richmond on government business. He had asked Lincoln not to go.

John Wilkes Booth was twenty-six years old, the most celebrated actor in America, and a Confederate sympathizer whose commitment to the Confederate cause had intensified as the war went against the Confederacy in ways that his original optimism had not anticipated.

He had not fought. This mattered to him — the failure to fight for the cause he believed in while other men were dying for it produced a guilt and a compensatory grandiosity that the people who knew him in the final months of his life noticed and remarked upon. He spoke about the Confederacy with the fervor of the uncommitted, the passion of someone who had not been tested by the experience of actually fighting and losing and watching comrades die, and who was therefore not yet disillusioned.

His original plan was not assassination. It was kidnapping.

The kidnapping conspiracy that Booth organized in the autumn and winter of 1864 was intended to capture Lincoln — to seize him during one of his many unguarded public appearances, spirit him southward into Confederate Virginia, and hold him as a hostage to force the Union government to resume the prisoner exchange program that Grant had suspended. It was not a fantastical scheme in its basic concept — Lincoln's security was genuinely inadequate, and the routes between Washington and Confederate Virginia were genuinely porous — but its execution required a level of coordination and capability that Booth's small group of conspirators, assembled through personal connection and shared sympathy rather than professional vetting, did not consistently possess.

The conspiracy to kidnap Lincoln evolved, in the final weeks of the war, into something darker and more violent as the military situation made kidnapping irrelevant. What purpose was served by holding Lincoln hostage to force prisoner exchanges when the Confederate armies were surrendering and the war was ending? Booth's answer — arrived at, the evidence suggests, in the days immediately following Lee's surrender at Appomattox — was to go further. Kill Lincoln. Kill Vice President Andrew Johnson simultaneously. Kill Secretary of State William Seward. Decapitate the Union government in a single night and create the chaos that might, somehow, allow the Confederate cause to recover from what had happened in Virginia.

It was not a coherent strategic plan. It was the plan of a man whose cause had been defeated and who was not willing to accept the defeat.

What Union intelligence knew about Booth and his circle in the months before April 14, 1865, is a question that the historical record answers only partially — and it is important to be precise about what that record establishes, because the gaps in it have been filled, over the 150 years since the assassination, with a remarkable quantity of speculation, fabrication, and conspiracy theory that has made the genuine intelligence failures harder to see clearly.

What is documented: Booth was known to Union counterintelligence as a Confederate sympathizer. He had been observed in the company of known Confederate agents and sympathizers in Washington and in the Maryland countryside where some of his co-conspirators lived. The Confederate covert action networks in Washington that Union counterintelligence monitored included individuals who moved in circles that overlapped with Booth's.

What is also documented: none of this intelligence produced any specific warning about a plot against Lincoln's life, or any action to increase Lincoln's security, in the weeks before April 14. Whether this reflects a failure to connect available information, a failure to prioritize the threat in the atmosphere of postwar relaxation, or simply the absence of specific intelligence about the specific plot is a question that the available evidence does not definitively resolve.

The documented intelligence that reached Union authorities in the period before April 14 included general warnings about threats to Lincoln — the kind of warnings that had been flowing to the White House since 1861 and that had been, through repetition and the absence of any specific interdiction, largely normalized. A general warning about threats to the president in a period when such warnings were routine did not generate the specific security response that a specific warning about a specific plot on a specific night might have generated.

This is not exculpation. It is description. The security apparatus was inadequate. The security culture was insufficiently serious about protecting a president who was himself insufficiently serious about being protected. These failures existed independently of any specific intelligence failure about Booth's specific plan.

Lafayette Charles Baker was the chief of the National Detective Police — the Union's primary counterintelligence and internal security organization — and he is one of the more difficult figures in the Civil War intelligence world to assess accurately.

He was, in certain respects, genuinely capable — a former San Francisco vigilante who had built the National Detective Police from a small operation into an organization of several hundred agents with a broad mandate for counterintelligence, internal security, and the suppression of fraud in government contracting. He was aggressive, ambitious, and not excessively concerned with the civil liberties of people he suspected of disloyalty — which made him both effective and deeply controversial, a combination that was not unusual in Civil War intelligence.

He was also, by multiple accounts, personally dishonest — running extortion operations through his own organization, profiting from the arrest and shakedown of people whose guilt was less important than their ability to pay for their freedom, and providing his superiors with intelligence assessments that reflected what he thought they wanted to hear rather than what the evidence actually supported.

Baker's role in the aftermath of the assassination — specifically, the pursuit and capture of Booth and the subsequent conspiracy trials — has been the subject of more historical controversy than his role in the intelligence failures that preceded it. He was not in Washington on the night of April 14 — he was in New York, and he returned to Washington after the assassination to take charge of the manhunt. His management of the pursuit of Booth, while it produced the eventual result — Booth was cornered and killed at the Garrett farm in Virginia on April 26 — involved enough operational irregularities and enough subsequent inconsistency in Baker's own accounts of what had happened to generate suspicion that has never been entirely satisfied.

The conspiracy theories about Lincoln's assassination that involve Baker — the suggestions that he was complicit in the plot, that he directed or enabled Booth, that he subsequently covered up evidence of a broader conspiracy — are not supported by the documentary evidence available to historians. What the documentary evidence does support is a picture of a man who was simultaneously genuinely effective in some aspects of his counterintelligence work and genuinely dishonest in his personal conduct, whose postwar memoir is so riddled with inconsistencies and fabrications that it cannot be used as a reliable source, and whose behavior in the aftermath of the assassination raised questions that were never adequately investigated.

Baker died in 1868, of meningitis, at forty-one. The questions died with him, unanswered.

The single police officer who was supposed to be protecting Abraham Lincoln on the night of April 14, 1865, was a Washington Metropolitan Police officer named John Frederick Parker.

Parker's record as a police officer was, to put it generously, undistinguished. He had been brought before the police board on multiple occasions for conduct unbecoming an officer — sleeping on duty, visiting a brothel while in uniform, conduct unrelated to the protection of anything or anyone. How he came to be assigned to the presidential detail is itself something of a mystery, though the mystery reflects less on any specific conspiracy than on the general inadequacy of the personnel systems governing executive protection in 1865.

On the night of April 14, Parker accompanied Lincoln to Ford's Theatre, showed Lincoln and his party to the state box, and then — at some point in the evening, by what accounts survive — left his post at the door of the box and went somewhere else. Whether he went to watch the play from a better vantage point, or to get a drink at the saloon next door to the theatre, or simply to sit in the corridor where he could not see the stage, is not established with certainty. What is established is that when John Wilkes Booth entered the state box at approximately 10:15 in the evening, there was no one at the door to stop him.

The derringer that Booth carried held a single ball. He had one shot. The distance between the gun and the back of Lincoln's head was about eighteen inches.

Parker was never prosecuted. He was brought before the police board in the days after the assassination and the charges were, for reasons that remain unexplained in the available records, dismissed. He continued to serve on the Washington Metropolitan Police until 1873, when he was finally dismissed — for sleeping on duty.

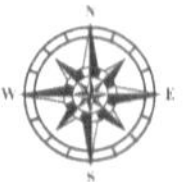

What conclusions does the documented record support about the intelligence failures that preceded Lincoln's assassination?

It supports the conclusion that the security culture surrounding Lincoln was chronically inadequate — that the normalization of threats, the president's own resistance to security measures, and the absence of any professional executive protection organization created conditions in which an assassination was, if not inevitable, significantly more likely than it should have been.

It supports the conclusion that Union counterintelligence knew enough about the Confederate covert action networks in Washington, and about individual figures connected to those networks, to have been more alert to specific threats than it apparently was in the weeks before April 14.

It does not support the conclusion — advanced by conspiracy theorists for 150 years — that the assassination was directed by Confederate President Jefferson Davis, or orchestrated by Secretary of War Edwin Stanton, or enabled by a deliberate decision to leave Lincoln unprotected. The evidence for these theories is not evidence in any serious sense. It is the accumulation of suspicion and anomaly and motivated inference that any sufficiently complex historical event generates, especially when the event is traumatic enough to resist the psychological acceptance that a simpler explanation might provide.

John Wilkes Booth killed Abraham Lincoln. He was motivated by Confederate sympathy, personal grandiosity, and the specific rage of a man who had watched his cause defeated and was not willing to accept the defeat. He was not directed by Jefferson Davis, who did not know what Booth was planning. He was not enabled by Stanton, who did not want Lincoln dead.

He was enabled by a security apparatus that was inadequate, a president who was philosophically resistant to being protected, a police officer who left his post, and a city that had spent ten days celebrating the end of a war and had, in that celebration, lowered its guard against the men who had not yet accepted that the war was over.

That is the documented record. It is damning enough without embellishment.

It is also, in its way, a final intelligence failure — the failure to maintain, in the moment of apparent victory, the vigilance that the situation still required.

The war was not over for everyone. Union intelligence did not know this. It should have.

THE RECKONING

What the Shadows Left Behind

What the Secret War Achieved and What It Cost

The war ended in courthouse and a theatre — at Appomattox on April 9, 1865, and at Ford's Theatre five days later — and the shadow war that had run alongside it ended in the same disorderly, unannounced way that it had been conducted: not with a formal conclusion but with a gradual cessation, the networks going quiet one by one, the agents coming in from the cold or not coming in at all, the files being closed or burned or simply abandoned in the offices of organizations that were dissolving around them.

There was no peace treaty for the secret war. There was no moment at which the intelligence services of both sides laid down their instruments and acknowledged what had been done. The men and women who had fought it simply stopped fighting it, or were stopped by circumstances — capture, execution, the ending of the cause they had served — and went back to whatever lives the war had left them.

What they had accomplished, and what it had cost them, deserves an accounting.

Not a triumphalist one. Not the kind of accounting that inflates contributions and smooths over failures and presents the shadow war as a clean story of American ingenuity and courage, which it was not, or not only. An honest one.

The strategic contribution of Civil War intelligence operations to the war's outcome is real but requires careful calibration.

The signal intelligence contribution at the First Battle of Bull Run — Alexander's flag message warning of the Union flanking movement — contributed to a Confederate victory that shaped the entire subsequent character of the war. If the message had not been sent, or had not been received in time, the Union flanking movement might have succeeded, the Confederate left might have collapsed, and the battle that became the first great shock of the war might have ended differently. The chain of counterfactuals is long and the certainties are few, but the contribution was real.

The railway sabotage that delayed the 2nd SS Panzer Division Das Reich — no, that is the wrong war. Stay here. The railway intelligence that Anson Stager's cipher system protected, the telegraph traffic that Charles Tinker decrypted in the War Department office while Lincoln read over his shoulder, the aerial intelligence that Thaddeus Lowe transmitted down the tether rope from five hundred feet above the Virginia Peninsula — these contributed, in ways that are documented if not always precisely quantifiable, to the Union's ability to manage a war of unprecedented scale and complexity.

The Confederate commerce raiding campaign — intelligence-enabled, operationally sophisticated, prosecuted by commanders who understood that knowing where your targets were was the prerequisite for finding them — inflicted damage on American maritime commerce that outlasted the war by decades. The American merchant marine never recovered its prewar position. The Alabama Claims that Britain eventually paid acknowledged, implicitly, that the Confederate intelligence network in Liverpool had produced consequences that neutral governments were legally obligated not to enable.

Elizabeth Van Lew's network in Richmond provided Grant with intelligence from inside the Confederate capital during the final year of the war. Allan Pinkerton's network provided McClellan with intelligence that was systematically wrong and that contributed to operational delays that cost the Union opportunities it could not recover. Both of these things are true. The intelligence services of both sides had their successes and their failures, and the honest accounting holds both.

The human cost of the shadow war is harder to calculate than its strategic impact, because it falls unevenly on people whose names the historical record has preserved with unevenly distributed care.

Timothy Webster was hanged in Richmond in April 1862, carried to the gallows on a chair because he was too ill to walk to his own execution. His name is in the history books — not prominently, but it is there. He can be found.

The African American scouts and intelligence gatherers who fed information to Union commanders throughout the war — the men and women whose invisibility was their operational asset and whose obscurity is their posthumous condition — are mostly not findable. The debriefing reports that document what they told Union officers name the officers and omit the sources. The operational intelligence they provided flows through the Union military record without attribution. They are present in the outcomes and absent from the acknowledgments, which is exactly the position that the society they were serving had assigned to them and which the military intelligence system they served had not yet learned to challenge.

Harriet Tubman's name is known, and the Combahee River Raid has received, in recent years, the historical attention it deserves. Mary Elizabeth Bowser's name is known, though the limits of the documentary record mean that the specific dimensions of her contribution to Van Lew's network cannot be established with the certainty that the story deserves. John Scobell's name is known primarily through Pinkerton's memoir, which is not a reliable source but is the only source there is.

The others — the unnamed scouts, the unnamed couriers, the unnamed people who carried intelligence through Confederate lines and across the lines of a society that had enslaved them — are not known. Their contributions to the Union war effort were real. Their absence from the historical record is also real, and it is a form of injustice that acknowledging it does not repair.

The women who served in the shadow war on both sides have fared somewhat better in the historical record, largely because their stories were dramatic enough to attract attention in ways that the quieter contributions of less spectacular operatives did not.

Rose O'Neal Greenhow's story has been told many times, shaped by the Confederate commemorative tradition that made her a heroine and by the more recent historical scholarship that has insisted on holding her cause alongside her effectiveness. Belle Boyd told her own story, for forty years and at considerable profit, in terms that mixed genuine experience with professional embellishment. Elizabeth Van Lew was rescued from obscurity by researchers who recognized, in the fragmentary record she left, the outlines of an operation that deserved far more attention than it had received.

The women whose contributions were less dramatic, whose intelligence work was conducted through the quiet accumulation of observed detail rather than through the theatrical gesture — the countless unnamed women who carried messages, sheltered agents, provided cover for operations they were never officially part of — are as invisible as their African American counterparts. The masculine mythology of the Lost Cause and the Grand Army of the Republic was not constructed to preserve the memory of women who had done unglamorous things without witnesses.

They did them anyway. The operations depended on them. The history mostly forgot them.

What the Civil War intelligence experience established for the future of American intelligence is one of the more consequential legacies of the conflict — and one of the least recognized.

The Military Telegraph Service and the cipher system that Anson Stager developed for it established the precedent for what we would now call signals intelligence — the interception, decryption, and exploitation of enemy communications as a systematic military function. The problems that the Civil War telegraph operators encountered — how to encrypt communications, how to detect when lines had been compromised, how to use intercepted enemy traffic operationally while protecting the fact of the interception — are problems that the intelligence services of the twentieth century would encounter again in more technologically sophisticated forms. The Civil War worked out the first American answers.

The Balloon Corps established the principle of aerial reconnaissance — the idea that getting above the battlefield and looking down was a fundamentally different intelligence capability from anything that could be done from the ground, and that the investment required to achieve that capability was worth making. The Corps was disbanded before its potential was fully realized, for reasons that had more to do with bureaucratic politics than operational judgment, and the United States Army would not have a systematic aerial reconnaissance capability again until the First World War. But the principle survived the institution that had demonstrated it, and the officers who had watched Lowe's balloons above the Virginia Peninsula carried the lesson into the postwar decades.

The Pinkerton organization — and its successor, Lafayette Baker's National Detective Police — established the precedent for a domestic counterintelligence capability: an organization dedicated to identifying and neutralizing threats to the Union government from within Union territory. The methods both organizations used were often legally dubious and personally dishonest. The precedent they established — that the federal government required a counterintelligence function that operated within the country's borders — survived their specific failures and their specific corruptions.

The Signal Corps that Albert Myer built established the precedent for a military communications organization — a dedicated corps of trained specialists whose function was not fighting but connecting, whose instruments were not weapons but wires and flags and eventually the full range of communications technologies that the following century would produce. The Signal Corps survived the war and survived Myer's removal from its command and survived the bureaucratic battles that had nearly ended it, and it became, in the postwar decades, the institutional foundation for American military communications.

The unresolved questions that the Civil War intelligence experience left for subsequent American conflicts are perhaps its most durable legacy.

The legal status of spies and covert operators — the question that had produced the executions of Timothy Webster and the Andrews Raiders and the anguished debates over what to do with Belle Boyd — was not resolved by the Civil War. It was complicated by it. The distinction between a spy, who could be executed, and a prisoner of war, who could not, turned on the question of whether the operative was in uniform — a distinction that subsequent conflicts would make progressively more complicated as the nature of warfare changed and the lines between combatant and civilian, between military and paramilitary, between state-directed and freelance intelligence operations became harder to draw.

The question of how to balance intelligence effectiveness against civil liberties — the question that the arrests of Copperhead leaders, the suspension of habeas corpus, and the operations of Baker's National Detective Police had raised — was similarly unresolved. The Civil War established that the federal government would, in conditions of extreme national emergency, exercise intelligence and counterintelligence powers that it did not formally possess in peacetime and that were in tension with constitutional protections that the war had not suspended. Every subsequent American conflict has revisited this tension and none has resolved it.

The question of how to use intelligence produced by sources whose humanity the system does not fully recognize — the question that the treatment of African American intelligence contributors had raised in its most acute form — was unresolved in 1865 and would remain unresolved, in various forms, through the subsequent history of American intelligence. The intelligence services of the twentieth century would struggle with versions of the same problem: how to use information from people whose status within the system that uses their information is not equal to the value of what they provide.

What was the shadow war, finally?

It was improvised. Both sides built their intelligence capabilities from nothing, in the first months of a conflict that no one had adequately prepared for, using whatever was available — commercial telegraph operators, civilian balloon aeronauts, private detective agencies, women whose social access substituted for institutional standing, enslaved people whose knowledge of the landscape they had been forced to inhabit was the most valuable intelligence asset either side possessed.

It was brilliant, in specific moments and specific operations — Alexander's flag at Bull Run, Tubman's network on the Combahee, Ellsworth's telegraph conversations while Morgan's men cut the line, Van Lew's cipher reports flowing from Richmond to Grant's headquarters at City Point.

It was brutal in the way that all intelligence work is brutal when the stakes are high enough — Webster carried to the gallows, the Andrews Raiders hanged in Atlanta, Sam Davis standing on the scaffold in Pulaski refusing to say the name that would have saved his life.

And it was consequential. Not decisive — wars are not won by intelligence services alone, and the Civil War was won by the Army of the Potomac and the Army of the Tennessee and the naval blockade and the industrial capacity of the Northern states and the political genius of Abraham Lincoln and the moral weight of the Emancipation Proclamation and a thousand other factors that intelligence supported but did not create. But consequential. The shadow war shaped specific outcomes at specific moments, preserved capabilities and threatened them, produced information that commanders needed and withheld information that their enemies needed, and established — in the process of doing all of this under pressure and without precedent — the institutional and doctrinal foundations of what would become, in the twentieth century, one of the most powerful intelligence establishments in the world.

The last Confederate commerce raider to surrender was the CSS Shenandoah, which lowered its flag in Liverpool harbor on November 6, 1865 — more than six months after Appomattox, three weeks after the last Confederate land forces had surrendered.

Her captain, James Waddell, had continued hunting Union whalers in the Pacific until August 1865, when a passing British vessel finally provided him with reliable news that the war had ended months before. He had been fighting a war that was over. He had not known.

There is something in this that captures the essential character of the shadow war — the intelligence that arrives too late, or not at all, or in a form that cannot be trusted or acted upon. Waddell was an intelligence failure's final victim: a capable officer, commanding a capable ship, whose effectiveness had been made possible by the Confederate naval intelligence network in the Atlantic ports — and whose continued operations after the war's end were made possible by the absence of the same.

He sailed into Liverpool and surrendered his ship and his crew to the British authorities, because there was no longer a Confederate government to surrender to. The war had ended. The shadow war had ended with it.

What remained was the record — incomplete, contested, systematically biased toward the experiences of the powerful and the documented — and the question of how to read it honestly.

The shadow war was fought by people who were mostly trying to do what they believed was right, in service of causes that history has judged with varying degrees of approval, using methods that ranged from the unambiguously heroic to the morally catastrophic. It was fought largely in the dark, by people who did not know how it would end or whether what they were doing would matter.

Some of it mattered enormously. Some of it mattered not at all. Most of it falls somewhere in between — real contributions to real outcomes, made by real people at real cost, in a war that reshaped the country that had to fight it.

That is the honest accounting.

It will have to be enough.

Glossary

T he Shadow Wars Series

The following glossary covers the key organizations, agencies, terms, and operational concepts that appear across the Shadow Wars Series. Entries are arranged alphabetically. Readers encountering an unfamiliar term while reading any volume in the series will find a plain-language explanation here.

A

A Force — British military deception unit based in Cairo during World War II, responsible for strategic deception operations in the Middle East and North Africa, including Operation Bertram, which contributed to the success of the Second Battle of El Alamein in 1942.

Abwehr — Germany's military intelligence service, operating from 1920 to 1944 under the German Armed Forces High Command. Responsible for espionage, counterintelligence, and sabotage operations. Disbanded by Hitler in 1944 and its functions absorbed by the SS and SD after Admiral Wilhelm Canaris, its longtime chief, fell under suspicion.

Agent — In intelligence terminology, a person who gathers information or performs operations on behalf of an intelligence service. Distinct from an "officer," who is a professional employee of the intelligence organization. An agent may be a foreign national, a recruited civilian, or anyone working under the direction of an intelligence service.

AK (Armia Krajowa) — The Home Army. The dominant Polish resistance movement during World War II, operating under the command of the Polish government-in-exile in London. At its peak one of the largest underground resistance organizations in occupied Europe, conducting sabotage, intelligence gathering, and armed operations against the German occupation.

Alliance Network — The largest French intelligence network of World War II, run by Marie-Madeleine Fourcade and known internally as Noah's Ark. Operated throughout the German occupation of France, providing extensive intelligence about German naval and military operations to British intelligence.

Armistice — A formal agreement to stop fighting, typically as a prelude to a peace treaty. In the context of this series, refers primarily to the armistice of November 11, 1918, ending World War I, and the armistice of June 22, 1940, between Germany and France following the German invasion, which established the Vichy French government.

Asset — An intelligence term for a person, organization, or resource that provides useful information or services to an intelligence operation. A human asset is a person providing intelligence or assistance, whether voluntarily, for payment, or under coercion.

Ausweis — A German identity document or pass, required under German occupation in much of Europe during World War II. Different types of Ausweis granted different levels of movement and access. The ability to produce a convincing forged Ausweis was critical to the survival of agents and Jews fleeing persecution in occupied Europe.

B

BCRA (Bureau Central de Renseignements et d'Action) — The Central Bureau of Intelligence and Operations. The Free French intelligence and special operations service, established in London in 1942 under the direction of General de Gaulle's government in exile. Coordinated French resistance intelligence activities and liaison with British SOE and American OSS.

Black propaganda — Disinformation or propaganda that conceals or misrepresents its true origin, typically making it appear to come from a source it does not. Used extensively by both Allied and Axis powers during World War II to undermine enemy morale, spread confusion, or manipulate enemy decision-making.

Blown — Intelligence slang for an agent or operation whose cover has been compromised and is known to the opposing intelligence service. A blown agent is in immediate danger and must be extracted or go into hiding. A blown operation must be abandoned.

Burned — Intelligence slang for an agent who has been identified by hostile counterintelligence and can no longer operate safely in a given environment. A burned agent may be deliberately exposed by their own service when they are no longer useful, or may be identified through their own mistakes or through enemy penetration of their network.

C

CIA (Central Intelligence Agency) — The United States' principal foreign intelligence service, established in 1947 as the successor to the wartime Office of Strategic Services (OSS). Responsible for collecting, analyzing, and disseminating foreign intelligence and conducting covert operations abroad. Headquartered in Langley, Virginia.

Cipher — A system for encrypting information by substituting or transposing letters or symbols according to a predetermined key. Distinguished from a code, in which entire words or phrases are replaced by other words or symbols. Ciphers were the primary method of securing military and intelligence communications throughout both World Wars and the Cold War.

Clandestine operation — An operation conducted in secret, with its existence concealed from those not involved. In intelligence terminology, distinguished from a covert operation, in which the operation may be acknowledged but the sponsoring organization is concealed.

Cold War — The period of geopolitical tension between the United States and its Western allies and the Soviet Union and its Eastern bloc partners, lasting from approximately 1947 to the dissolution of the Soviet Union in 1991. Characterized by ideological conflict, proxy wars, nuclear arms race, and extensive espionage by both sides, but no direct military conflict between the superpowers.

Compartmentalization — A security practice in which information is divided into separate compartments, with each person or unit knowing only what is necessary for their specific function. Standard practice in intelligence operations to limit the damage caused by the capture or betrayal of any individual agent.

Composition C (C-4) — A plastic explosive compound developed in Britain during World War II and used extensively by SOE agents and resistance networks for sabotage operations. The predecessor of modern C-4 explosive. Its plasticity allowed it to be shaped to fit specific targets, making it far more versatile than earlier explosive compounds.

Counterintelligence — Intelligence activities designed to identify, neutralize, and exploit the intelligence operations of foreign powers or hostile organizations. Includes surveillance of suspected agents, penetration of enemy intelligence services, and the running of double agents.

Courier — A person who physically transports intelligence materials, documents, or other sensitive items between agents or between agents and their handlers. Courier work is among the most dangerous functions in a clandestine network, as capture means arrest with incriminating materials in hand.

Cover — A false identity or explanation adopted by an agent to conceal their true purpose or affiliation. A cover story is the explanation an agent provides for their presence, activities, or identity. Cover may be shallow (a simple false name) or deep (a fully constructed false biography supported by forged documents and a verifiable history).

Covert operation — An operation in which the sponsoring organization's involvement is concealed, even if the operation itself may eventually become known. Distinct from a clandestine operation, in which both the operation and its sponsorship are secret.

Croix de Guerre — A French military decoration established during World War I and awarded for acts of valor in the presence of enemy forces. One of the highest French military honors, awarded to numerous resistance fighters, SOE agents, and intelligence operatives including Virginia Hall and Josephine Baker.

D

D-Day — Military terminology for the day on which a combat operation begins. In common usage, refers specifically to June 6, 1944, the date of the Allied amphibious landings in Normandy, France — the largest seaborne invasion in history, which opened the Western Front against Germany.

Dead drop — A method of passing intelligence materials between agents without direct personal contact. Materials are left at a prearranged location (the "drop") by one party and collected by another, reducing the risk that both parties will be observed together. Widely used during the Cold War.

Defector — A person who abandons their country, cause, or allegiance, typically to join or provide information to an opposing power. Intelligence defectors are particularly valuable because they bring firsthand knowledge of the organizations they have left.

Deuxième Bureau — The Second Bureau. France's military intelligence service, operating throughout World War I and into World War II. Responsible for foreign intelligence collection and analysis. Effectively dissolved after the fall of France in 1940, with its functions split between Vichy French intelligence and the Free French BCRA.

Direction finding (DF) — A technique for locating a radio transmitter by triangulating its signal using multiple receiving stations or mobile units. German direction-finding vans were a primary threat to clandestine radio operators in occupied Europe during World War II. A transmitting agent typically had twenty minutes to two hours before direction-finding equipment could pinpoint their location.

Double agent — An agent who ostensibly works for one intelligence service while secretly working for another. Double agents may be genuine defectors who maintain contact with their original service, agents who have been turned after capture, or agents deliberately planted to deceive the opposing service. Among the most valuable and dangerous figures in intelligence operations.

DS (Durzhavna Sigurnost) — The Bulgarian State Security service, the communist-era intelligence and secret police organization of Bulgaria. Closely aligned with the KGB and responsible for several Cold War-era operations in Western Europe, including the 1978 assassination of Bulgarian dissident Georgi Markov in London.

E

Electric Fence (High Voltage Fence) — The electrified wire barrier erected by the German occupation authorities along the Belgian-Dutch and Franco-Belgian borders during World War I and again during World War II. Designed to prevent the unauthorized movement of people and information across the frontier. The fence was lethal and claimed the lives of numerous agents and civilians attempting to cross.

Englandspiel — The England Game. A German Abwehr deception operation conducted in the Netherlands from 1942 to 1944, in which captured SOE agents were forced to transmit back to London under German control. The operation resulted in fifty-four Allied agents being sent into German-controlled territory and captured on arrival. One of the most successful counterintelligence operations of World War II.

Exfiltration — The clandestine removal of an agent or other person from a hostile or denied area. The covert equivalent of evacuation. Exfiltration routes during World War II typically ran through neutral countries such as Spain, Sweden, or Switzerland.

F

F Section — The French Section of the British Special Operations Executive, responsible for operations in France independent of the Free French government-in-exile. Distinct from the RF Section, which coordinated with the Free French. F Section deployed over 400 agents into France during World War II, including many of the women whose stories appear in this series.

FBI (Federal Bureau of Investigation) — The United States' domestic intelligence and law enforcement agency, responsible for counterintelligence within US borders. During World War II, the FBI under J. Edgar Hoover was responsible for identifying enemy agents operating in the United States, including the investigation of Velvalee Dickinson's doll code operation.

Free French — The French government-in-exile and its associated military forces, established by General Charles de Gaulle in London following the fall of France in June 1940. Continued the fight against Germany from abroad and coordinated with the French resistance inside occupied France through the BCRA.

Fuze (or Fuse) — A device used to detonate an explosive charge after a set period of time or upon specific stimulus. In SOE and OSS sabotage operations, time-delay fuzes allowed agents to set charges and leave the area before detonation. The reliability of the fuze was critical — an early detonation killed the agent, a late one gave the enemy time to find and disarm the charge.

G

George Cross (GC) — The second-highest British civilian decoration, awarded for acts of the greatest heroism or most conspicuous courage in circumstances of extreme danger. Awarded posthumously to Noor Inayat Khan and Violette Szabo, among other SOE agents.

Gestapo (Geheime Staatspolizei) — The Secret State Police of Nazi Germany, established in 1933. Responsible for investigating and suppressing resistance and opposition to the Nazi regime. In occupied Europe, the Gestapo was the primary threat to resistance networks and Allied agents, known for brutal interrogation methods and the systematic arrest and execution of captured operatives.

GRU (Glavnoye Razvedyvatelnoye Upravleniye) — The Main Intelligence Directorate of the Soviet Armed Forces. The Soviet military intelligence service, distinct from the civilian KGB and its predecessors. Throughout the Cold War, the GRU ran extensive networks of agents in Western countries focused on military and technical intelligence. Officers of the GRU include Ruth Werner (codename Sonya) and the members of the Richard Sorge spy ring.

H

Handler — An intelligence officer responsible for managing and directing an agent or network of agents. The handler provides instructions, receives intelligence, arranges communication, and is responsible for the agent's security and welfare. The handler–agent relationship is the fundamental operational unit of human intelligence collection.

Honey trap (also: honey pot) — An intelligence operation in which a romantic or sexual relationship is used to compromise, recruit, or extract information from a target. Used by multiple intelligence services throughout the period covered by this series. The KGB's systematic use of female officers in this role gave rise to the term "Swallow" for female operatives and "Raven" for male ones.

I

Illegal — In Soviet intelligence terminology, an officer or agent operating in a foreign country without diplomatic cover, using a false identity and without the protection of diplomatic immunity. Distinct from a "legal," who operates under diplomatic cover. Illegals are more difficult to identify but face severe consequences if captured, as they have no official status to protect them.

Infiltration — The covert insertion of an agent or agents into enemy-held territory or into a target organization. During World War II, SOE and OSS agents were typically infiltrated into occupied Europe by parachute, by small boat, or by crossing land borders using false identity documents.

Intelligence — Information that has been collected, analyzed, and evaluated for use by decision-makers. In military and governmental contexts, intelligence refers both to the information itself and to the organizations and processes that produce it. Raw information becomes intelligence through the process of analysis and assessment.

Invisible ink — A substance used to write messages that are invisible under normal conditions but can be revealed through application of heat, light, or a chemical developer. Used throughout the period covered by this series to conceal intelligence messages in apparently innocent correspondence. Josephine Baker used invisible ink to write intelligence on her sheet music.

Iron Curtain — The political, military, and ideological boundary dividing Europe between the Western democratic nations and the Soviet-dominated Eastern bloc during the Cold War. The term was popularized by Winston Churchill in a 1946 speech. Along the Iron Curtain's physical manifestations — the Berlin Wall, the fortified borders between East and West — much of the Cold War's human drama played out.

J

Jedburgh teams — Three-person teams of Allied officers (typically one American, one British, and one French) parachuted into occupied France ahead of the D-Day landings to organize, train, and coordinate resistance operations.

Named after the Scottish town where they trained. Operated in coordination with both SOE and OSS.

K

Kamera — Also known as Special Bureau Number One. The KGB laboratory responsible for developing poisons and other assassination compounds for use in Soviet intelligence operations. Established under Stalin and continued in various forms through the Soviet period. Responsible for the ricin pellet used to assassinate Bulgarian dissident Georgi Markov in London in 1978.

KGB (Komitet Gosudarstvennoy Bezopasnosti) — The Committee for State Security. The Soviet Union's principal security and intelligence agency from 1954 to 1991, responsible for both foreign intelligence collection and domestic security. The KGB was the successor to a series of earlier Soviet security organizations including the NKVD, NKGB, and MGB. Dissolved following the collapse of the Soviet Union in 1991, its functions divided among successor organizations including the FSB and SVR.

Kennkarte — The German identity card issued to inhabitants of occupied territories during World War II, containing the bearer's name, date and place of birth, physical description, photograph, thumbprint, and signature. One of the primary documents that Allied forgers worked to replicate. A convincing forged Kennkarte was essential to any agent operating under cover in German-occupied Europe.

L

La Dame Blanche — The White Lady. A Belgian and French intelligence network of approximately 1,000 agents that operated during World War I, providing British military intelligence with extensive information about German troop and railway movements through systematic observation. One of the most productive Allied intelligence networks of the war, with women constituting a significant portion of its membership.

Légion d'honneur — The Legion of Honor. France's highest order of merit, established by Napoleon Bonaparte in 1802. Awarded to military personnel and civilians for exceptional service to France. Received by several subjects of this series including Virginia Hall, Josephine Baker, and Marie-Madeleine Fourcade.

Limpet mine — A type of naval mine attached to a ship's hull by magnets, detonated by a time-delay fuze. Developed by SOE's Station IX and used extensively by Allied frogmen and resistance operatives to sink or damage enemy shipping without direct combat. The name derives from the limpet shellfish, which attaches firmly to rocks.

M

Manhattan Project — The American-led research and development program, conducted during World War II with British and Canadian participation, that produced the world's first nuclear weapons. Operated from 1942 to 1946 under conditions of extreme secrecy. Soviet intelligence penetration of the Manhattan Project — primarily through the networks of Klaus Fuchs, Julius Rosenberg, and others — provided the Soviet Union with significant technical information that accelerated its own nuclear weapons program.

MBE (Member of the Order of the British Empire) — A British honor awarded for significant achievement or service to the community. Among the lower tier of the Order of the British Empire. Awarded to Christine Granville (Krystyna Skarbek) for her wartime service, alongside the George Cross and the Croix de Guerre.

MI5 (Military Intelligence, Section 5) — The United Kingdom's domestic counterintelligence and security agency, formally known as the Security Service. Responsible for identifying and neutralizing threats to British national security from within the United Kingdom, including foreign intelligence operations on British soil. During World War II, MI5 ran the Double Cross System, turning captured German agents into double agents.

MI6 (Military Intelligence, Section 6) — The United Kingdom's foreign intelligence service, formally known as the Secret Intelligence Service (SIS). Responsible for collecting intelligence outside the United Kingdom. Distinct from MI5, which handles domestic security. The organization whose wartime penetration by Kim Philby represents one of the Cold War's most damaging intelligence failures.

Microfilm — A photographic technique that reduces documents or images to a tiny fraction of their original size, allowing large amounts of information to be concealed in very small objects. Widely used in Cold War intelligence operations to pass classified documents. The hollow nickel used by Soviet spy Rudolf Abel contained a microfilm image.

Mitrokhin Archive — A collection of handwritten notes and transcriptions of KGB files made secretly by KGB archivist Vasili Mitrokhin over a period of years and brought to Britain when he defected in 1992. The archive provided Western intelligence services with an unprecedented view into KGB operations spanning decades. Published in two volumes by Christopher Andrew and Vasili Mitrokhin as The Mitrokhin Archive (1999) and The Mitrokhin Archive II (2005).

Mole — An agent who has penetrated an enemy organization from within, typically by being recruited before joining the target organization or very early in their career. Distinguished from a defector or walk-in by the long-term, premeditated nature of the penetration. The Cambridge Spy

Ring represents the most famous example of mole penetration in British intelligence history.

N

Nacht und Nebel (Night and Fog) — A directive issued by Hitler in December 1941, ordering that certain prisoners — primarily resistance fighters and spies from occupied Western Europe — be made to "disappear" into the German security apparatus without any information being provided to their families or governments. Nacht und Nebel prisoners were typically transported to concentration camps in Germany, kept in isolation, and their fates kept secret. Noor Inayat Khan was classified as a Nacht und Nebel prisoner.

Network — In intelligence terminology, an organized group of agents working together under common direction to collect intelligence or conduct operations. Also called a circuit or cell structure. Most resistance and intelligence networks were compartmentalized so that the arrest of one member could not reveal the entire network.

NKVD (Narodnyy Komissariat Vnutrennikh Del) — The People's Commissariat for Internal Affairs. A Soviet security and intelligence organization that served multiple functions including secret police, intelligence collection, and administration of the Gulag labor camp system. The NKVD's foreign intelligence functions were among its most significant activities during the 1930s and 1940s. Reorganized multiple times and eventually replaced by the KGB in 1954.

O

Office of Strategic Services (OSS) — The United States' wartime intelligence and special operations agency, established in 1942 under the direction of General William "Wild Bill" Donovan. The OSS conducted intelligence collection, analysis, sabotage, and subversion operations in both the European and Pacific theaters. Dissolved at the end of World War II, its functions eventually transferred to the newly created CIA in 1947.

Official Secrets Act — British legislation criminalizing the unauthorized disclosure of information related to national security or intelligence activities. The Official Secrets Act bound all SOE and MI6 personnel and agents, preventing them from publicly discussing their wartime activities for decades after the war. Many participants in the events described in this series carried their knowledge in silence for the rest of their lives as a direct result of this legislation.

One-time pad — An encryption system in which the key used to encrypt a message is as long as the message itself and is used only once. When properly implemented, the one-time pad is mathematically unbreakable. Used by Soviet intelligence for communication with agents in the field. The hollow nickel used by Rudolf Abel contained a one-time pad key in microfilm form.

Operation Bernhard — The Nazi program to destabilize the British economy by flooding it with forged Bank of England notes, executed using Jewish prisoners at Sachsenhausen concentration camp from 1942 to 1945. Produced between £130 million and £150 million in forged notes. Named after its supervisor, SS officer Bernhard Krüger.

Operation Mincemeat — A British deception operation conducted in 1943, in which the corpse of a homeless Welsh man was dressed as a British Royal Marines officer and floated off the coast of Spain carrying forged documents suggesting Allied plans to invade Greece and Sardinia rather than Sicily. The deception succeeded in misleading German intelligence about the actual Allied invasion target.

Operation Torch — The Allied invasion of French North Africa in November 1942, the first major Allied offensive in the Western theater. The operation's success was aided by intelligence gathered by OSS agent Amy Thorpe, whose acquisition of Vichy French naval ciphers gave Allied planners critical information about French naval dispositions.

P

Penetration — The successful insertion of an agent into a target organization for the purpose of collecting intelligence or conducting influence operations from within. The penetration of Allied intelligence networks by German counter-intelligence — and the penetration of Western intelligence services by Soviet agents — are central themes throughout this series.

Plastic explosive — An explosive compound with a clay-like consistency that can be shaped by hand to fit specific targets. Its malleability makes it far more versatile than rigid explosive compounds for sabotage applications. Composition C (the British formulation) and its successor C-4 (the American formulation) were the standard plastic explosives used by SOE and OSS operatives.

Propaganda — Information, especially of a biased or misleading nature, used to promote a particular political cause or point of view. Both Allied and Axis powers invested heavily in propaganda operations during World War II, targeting both civilian populations and military personnel. White propaganda acknowledges its source; black propaganda disguises or misrepresents it.

R

Radio game — A deception operation in which a captured agent's radio is operated by the capturing intelligence service to feed false information to the agent's original handlers. The German Englandspiel operation in the Netherlands is the most extensively documented example of this technique during World War II.

Raven — KGB terminology for a male intelligence officer used in seduction operations against female targets. The female equivalent was called a Swallow. Part of the systematic KGB program using personal relationships as an intelligence tool against Western targets.

Resistance — Organized opposition to enemy occupation or control. During World War II, resistance movements operated throughout German-occupied Europe, conducting intelligence collection, sabotage, escape line operations, and eventually armed action against the occupying forces. Resistance networks were supplied and supported by SOE and OSS and were central to Allied intelligence collection efforts.

Ricin — A highly toxic compound derived from castor beans, with no known antidote. Used by the KGB in the 1978 assassination of Bulgarian dissident Georgi Markov in London, delivered via a platinum pellet fired from a modified umbrella. One of the most lethal naturally occurring poisons known.

S

Sabotage — Deliberate destruction of or damage to an enemy's equipment, infrastructure, or resources. A primary function of SOE and OSS operations in occupied Europe during World War II, targeting railways, industrial facilities, communications infrastructure, and military equipment to disrupt German war production and logistics.

SD (Sicherheitsdienst) — The Security Service of the SS, serving as the intelligence agency of the Nazi Party and the SS. Responsible for gathering intelligence about threats to the regime and, in occupied territories, identifying and suppressing resistance activities. The SD worked closely with the Gestapo in occupied Europe.

Security check — A prearranged signal embedded in an agent's radio transmissions to indicate that they are operating freely and not under enemy control. If the security check was absent from a transmission, it was supposed to alert the receiving station that the agent had been captured and was transmitting under duress. Failures to act on absent security checks contributed to several intelligence disasters during World War II.

SOE (Special Operations Executive) — Britain's clandestine sabotage and intelligence organization, established in 1940 on Churchill's instruction to "set Europe ablaze." The SOE trained and inserted agents into occupied Europe and Asia to conduct sabotage, support resistance networks, and gather intelligence. Employed both men and women as agents, and was at the forefront of developing the tools and techniques of covert warfare. Dissolved in 1946.

Sorge Ring — The Soviet spy network operated by Richard Sorge in Shanghai and subsequently in Tokyo from the early 1930s until its discovery in 1941. One of the most productive Soviet intelligence operations of the period, providing Moscow with critical information about Japanese and German military intentions. Agnes Smedley assisted in establishing the network's Shanghai phase.

SS (Schutzstaffel) — The Protection Squadron. Originally Hitler's personal bodyguard unit, the SS grew into a vast military, police, and administrative organization that was central to the operation of the Nazi state and the Holocaust. The SS encompassed the Gestapo, the SD, the concentration camp system, and the Waffen-SS military units, among other functions.

Station IX — The SOE's primary research and development facility, housed at The Frythe, a converted country hotel in Welwyn, Hertfordshire. The site where the suitcase radios, explosive coal, concealment devices, and other tools of the secret war were designed, built, and tested. Operated throughout World War II under conditions of strict secrecy.

Sten gun — A British submachine gun developed in 1941 and manufactured in large quantities for distribution to resistance networks and Allied forces. Deliberately designed for simplicity and cheapness, the Sten could be produced with minimal tooling and could be disassembled into components small enough to be carried covertly. Its reliability was variable, but its availability and concealability made it the primary weapon of the European resistance.

Swallow — KGB terminology for a female intelligence officer used in seduction operations against male targets. The male equivalent was called a Raven. The KGB's Second Chief Directorate maintained a systematic program using both Swallows and Ravens to compromise or recruit Western officials in Moscow and elsewhere during the Cold War.

T

Tradecraft — The techniques and methods used by intelligence officers and agents to conduct their operations while avoiding detection. Includes methods of communication, surveillance detection, cover maintenance, dead drop procedures, and the full range of operational skills required for clandestine work.

Triangulation — The process of determining the location of a radio transmitter by taking directional readings from two or more receiving points and finding their intersection. The basis of the direction-finding operations used by German security services to locate clandestine radio operators in occupied Europe.

Tube Alloys — The British wartime nuclear weapons research program, the predecessor of the joint British-American effort that became the Manhattan Project. Tube Alloys research produced technical information that was passed to Soviet intelligence by agents including Melita Norwood and Klaus Fuchs.

Turned agent — An agent who has been captured by an opposing intelligence service and persuaded or coerced to work for that service, typically by continuing to operate against their original employers under the direction of the capturing service. Mathilde Carré (La Chatte) is among the most documented examples of a turned agent in the World War II period.

U

U-boat (Unterseeboot) — German submarine. U-boats conducted an extended campaign against Allied shipping in the Atlantic throughout World War II, threatening to cut Britain's supply lines. Intelligence about U-boat operations, gathered in part through agents like Marthe Richer, was critical to Allied efforts to counter the submarine campaign.

V

Venona — A long-running US signals intelligence program that intercepted and decrypted Soviet intelligence communications between 1943 and 1980. The Venona decrypts identified numerous Soviet agents operating in the United States and Britain during and after World War II, including Klaus Fuchs, the Rosenbergs, and others. Declassified and released publicly beginning in 1995.

Vichy France — The French government established following France's defeat by Germany in June 1940, based in the spa town of Vichy and governing the unoccupied southern zone of France under the leadership of Marshal Philippe Pétain. The Vichy government collaborated with the German occupation in numerous respects, including implementing anti-Jewish legislation and cooperating with German intelligence operations. Ended with the Allied liberation of France in 1944.

W

Welrod — A suppressed bolt-action pistol developed at SOE's Station IX for use in close-range assassination and elimination operations. Its report was approximately equivalent to a handclap, making it suitable for indoor use without alerting nearby personnel. Issued to SOE agents and resistance fighters across occupied Europe and Southeast Asia, and remained in production in various classified contexts for decades after the war.

Wireless operator — An agent trained to operate a clandestine radio set for communication between a field network and its headquarters. Among the most dangerous roles in any resistance or intelligence network, as radio transmissions could be located by direction-finding equipment. The average life expectancy of an SOE wireless operator in France in 1943 was approximately six weeks.

World War I (The Great War) — The global conflict of 1914 to 1918, fought primarily in Europe between the Allied Powers (Britain, France, Russia, and later the United States) and the Central Powers (Germany, Austria-Hungary, and the Ottoman Empire). The first industrialized war on a global scale, and the conflict in which modern military intelligence, including systematic use of female agents, was first extensively developed.

World War II (The Second World War) — The global conflict of 1939 to 1945, fought between the Allied powers (Britain, the Soviet Union, the United States, and others) and the

Axis powers (Germany, Italy, and Japan). The largest and deadliest conflict in human history, and the period in which modern intelligence operations — including the systematic use of agents, sabotage networks, deception operations, and signals intelligence — reached their full development.

A Note On Sources

T raitors, *Spies, and Secret Agents* is a work of narrative nonfiction. Every person, event, operation, and organization described in this book is real. No characters have been invented, no dialogue fabricated, and no events dramatized beyond what the historical record supports. Where the historical record is contested, uncertain, or incomplete, those limitations are acknowledged directly in the text rather than smoothed over in the interest of a cleaner narrative.

The primary sources for this book draw on the Official Records of the War of the Rebellion — the massive multivolume compilation of Union and Confederate military correspondence, orders, and reports published by the United States War Department between 1880 and 1901 — as well as on the records of the United States Military Telegraph Service, the records of the National Detective Police, and the Signal Corps records held at the National Archives in Washington. Confederate records, which survived the war in more fragmentary condition than their Union counterparts, are supplemented by the postwar memoirs and testimony of Confederate officers and officials, which must be read with appropriate awareness of the commemorative and self-justificatory purposes they often served.

I have drawn extensively on the published historical scholarship listed in the bibliography that follows, as well as on firsthand accounts written by participants including Allan Pinkerton, Edward Porter Alexander, Raphael Semmes, James Bulloch, Belle Boyd, Fitzroy Maclean — no, wrong book. The firsthand accounts for this volume include Pinkerton's memoirs, Alexander's *Military Memoirs of a Confederate*, Bulloch's *The Secret Service of the Confederate States in Europe*, and the postwar testimony of Signal Corps officers and telegraph operators collected in the decades after the war.

The historical record for Black intelligence operatives during the Civil War is, to put it plainly, a disaster. Enslaved and free Black men and women took extraordinary risks to pass information — often at greater personal cost than any white operative faced — and the official record largely ignored them while they were doing it and forgot them afterward. Some of that was wartime secrecy. Most of it was something less forgivable. Where the record is thin, this book says so. Where it's gone entirely, that absence is treated as evidence in its own right — because who gets remembered and who doesn't is never an accident.

Readers who wish to pursue any of the operations, individuals, or organizations described in this book will find the bibliography a reliable starting point for further research.

Bibliography

General Works on the Civil War

Donald, David Herbert. *Lincoln*. Simon & Schuster, 1995.

Foote, Shelby. *The Civil War: A Narrative*. Three volumes. Random House, 1958-1974.

McPherson, James M. *Battle Cry of Freedom: The Civil War Era*. Oxford University Press, 1988.

Symonds, Craig L. *The Civil War at Sea*. Oxford University Press, 2012.

Ward, Geoffrey C. *The Civil War: An Illustrated History*. Knopf, 1990.

Union Intelligence and the Secret Service

Fishel, Edwin C. *The Secret War for the Union: The Untold Story of Military Intelligence in the Civil War*. Houghton Mifflin, 1996.

Pinkerton, Allan. *The Spy of the Rebellion: Being a True History of the Spy System of the United States Army During the Late Rebellion*. G.W. Carleton, 1883.

Pinkerton, Allan. *The Detective and the Somnambulist / The Murderer and the Fortune Teller*. W.B. Keen, Cooke & Co., 1875.

Recko, Corey. *A Spy for the Union: The Life and Execution of Timothy Webster*. McFarland, 2013.

Whiteman, Maxwell. *While Lincoln Lay Dying*. Union League of Philadelphia, 1968.

Confederate Intelligence and Covert Operations

Beymer, William Gilmore. *On Hazardous Service: Scouts and Spies of the North and South*. Harper & Brothers, 1912.

Bulloch, James D. *The Secret Service of the Confederate States in Europe*. Two volumes. Richard Bentley & Son, 1883.

Gaddy, David Winfred. *The Confederate Signal Corps*. University of Alabama Press, 1993.

Jones, Virgil Carrington. *Eight Hours Before Richmond*. Henry Holt, 1957.

Tidwell, William A. *Come Retribution: The Confederate Secret Service and the Assassination of Lincoln*. University Press of Mississippi, 1988.

Female Spies and Intelligence Operatives

Boyd, Belle. *Belle Boyd in Camp and Prison*. Blelock & Company, 1865.

Faust, Drew Gilpin. *Mothers of Invention: Women of the Slaveholding South in the American Civil War*. University of North Carolina Press, 1996.

Leonard, Elizabeth D. *All the Daring of the Soldier: Women of the Civil War Armies*. Norton, 1999.

Ryan, David D. *A Yankee Spy in Richmond: The Civil War Diary of "Crazy Bet" Van Lew*. Stackpole Books, 1996.

Varon, Elizabeth R. *Southern Lady, Yankee Spy: The True Story of Elizabeth Van Lew, a Union Agent in the Heart of the Confederacy.* Oxford University Press, 2003.

African American Intelligence and the Union War Effort

Clinton, Catherine. *Harriet Tubman: The Road to Freedom.* Little, Brown, 2004.

Foner, Eric. *The Fiery Trial: Abraham Lincoln and American Slavery.* Norton, 2010.

Larson, Kate Clifford. *Bound for the Promised Land: Harriet Tubman, Portrait of an American Hero.* Ballantine Books, 2004.

Sernett, Milton C. *Harriet Tubman: Myth, Memory, and History.* Duke University Press, 2007.

Taylor, Susie King. *Reminiscences of My Life in Camp.* Published by the author, 1902.

Cryptography and Communications Intelligence

Gaddy, David Winfred. *Confederate Signals and Secret Service.* Munsell, 1986.

Plum, William R. *The Military Telegraph During the Civil War in the United States.* Two volumes. Jansen, McClurg & Company, 1882.

Rosen, R.D. *Signal and Noise: A History of Military Cryptography.* Scribner, 2014.

The Signal Corps and Aerial Intelligence

Evans, Charles M. *War of the Aeronauts: A History of Ballooning During the Civil War.* Stackpole Books, 2002.

Haydon, F. Stansbury. *Aeronautics in the Union and Confederate Armies.* Johns Hopkins Press, 1941.

Scheips, Paul J. *The Military Telegraph in the Civil War*. Office of the Chief of Military History, 1983.

The Copperhead Movement and Internal Security

Klement, Frank L. *Dark Lanterns: Secret Political Societies, Conspiracies, and Treason Trials in the Civil War*. Louisiana State University Press, 1984.

Klement, Frank L. *The Copperheads in the Middle West*. University of Chicago Press, 1960.

Milton, George Fort. *Abraham Lincoln and the Fifth Column*. Vanguard Press, 1942.

Silbey, Joel H. *A Respectable Minority: The Democratic Party in the Civil War Era*. Norton, 1977.

Confederate Naval Intelligence and Commerce Raiding

Hearn, Chester G. *Gray Raiders of the Sea: How Eight Confederate Warships Destroyed the Union's High Seas Commerce*. International Marine Publishing, 1992.

Semmes, Raphael. *Memoirs of Service Afloat During the War Between the States*. Kelly, Piet & Company, 1869.

Sinclair, Arthur. *Two Years on the Alabama*. Lee and Shepard, 1895.

Taylor, John M. *Confederate Raider: Raphael Semmes of the Alabama*. Brassey's, 1994.

Espionage, Double Agents, and Turned Operatives

Bakeless, John. *Spies of the Confederacy*. J.B. Lippincott, 1970.

Bakeless, John. *Turncoats, Traitors and Heroes: Espionage in the American Revolution*. J.B. Lippincott, 1959.

Horan, James D. *Confederate Agent: A Discovery in History*. Crown Publishers, 1954.

Andrews' Raid and Special Operations

O'Neill, Charles. *Wild Train: The Story of the Andrews Raiders*. Random House, 1956.

Pittenger, William. *Daring and Suffering: A History of the Great Railroad Adventure*. J.W. Daughaday, 1863.

Witt, John Fabian. *Lincoln's Code: The Laws of War in American History*. Free Press, 2012.

The Assassination of Lincoln

Good, Timothy S. *We Saw Lincoln Shot: One Hundred Eyewitness Accounts*. University Press of Mississippi, 1995.

Hatch, Frederick. *Protecting President Lincoln: The Security Effort, the Thwarted Plots and the Disaster at Ford's Theatre*. McFarland, 2011.

Kauffman, Michael W. *American Brutus: John Wilkes Booth and the Lincoln Conspiracies*. Random House, 2004.

Swanson, James L. *Manhunt: The 12-Day Chase for Lincoln's Killer*. William Morrow, 2006.

Recommended Further Reading

For readers wishing to explore the broader history of Civil War intelligence and American espionage, the following works are particularly recommended:

Budiansky, Stephen. *Her Majesty's Spymaster: Elizabeth I, Sir Francis Walsingham, and the Birth of Modern Espionage*. Viking, 2005.

Feis, William B. *Grant's Secret Service: The Intelligence War from Belmont to Appomattox.* University of Nebraska Press, 2002.

Latimer, Jon. *Deception in War: The Art of the Bluff, the Value of Deceit, and the Most Thrilling Episodes of Cunning in Military History.* Overlook Press, 2001.

Mackintyre, Ben. *Double Cross: The True Story of the D-Day Spies.* Crown, 2012.

Rose, P.K. *The Civil War: Black American Contributions to Union Intelligence.* Center for the Study of Intelligence, Central Intelligence Agency, 1998.

Acknowledgements

A book about the intelligence history of the Civil War stands on the shoulders of scholars who spent careers in the archives that most historians pass through and move on from. The work of Edwin Fishel — whose *The Secret War for the Union* remains the most thorough treatment of Union military intelligence in the Civil War — shaped this book's understanding of what the intelligence services of both sides actually accomplished, as distinct from what the postwar memoirs claimed they accomplished. The distinction matters enormously, and Fishel drew it with a precision that this author has tried to honor.

The scholarship of Elizabeth Varon on Elizabeth Van Lew, of Kate Clifford Larson and Catherine Clinton on Harriet Tubman, and of Frank Klement on the Copperhead movement provided the historical foundation for chapters that required careful navigation of contested and sometimes politically charged territory. Where this book reaches different conclusions from these scholars, it does so with full awareness of the debt it owes them.

The records of the National Archives, the Library of Congress, and the collections of the various Civil War museums and historical societies that have preserved the documentary record of the conflict are the bedrock on which all Civil War scholarship rests. The archivists and librarians who maintain those collections deserve acknowledgment that the published histories they enable rarely provide.

This book is published under the Crazy Dog Publishing imprint, and would not exist without the readers of the Shadow Wars Series whose enthusiasm for narrative history of covert operations continues to grow.

Finally — the men and women whose stories fill these pages deserve the last word in any acknowledgment. They fought a secret war inside the most catastrophic conflict in American history, at costs that ranged from social ostracism to execution, for causes that history has judged with varying degrees of approval. Their courage was real regardless of the causes it served. Their contributions to the history of American intelligence — as practitioners, as innovators, as the people who worked out, under fire, how this kind of war was conducted — deserve to be remembered with the specificity and the honesty that they earned.

This book is an attempt at that remembrance.

Chuck Watson

Crazy Dog Publishing

Also by Chuck Watson

Shadow Armies: *The Secret Resistance Networks That Crippled Hitler's War Machine*

The Shadow Wars Series • Book One

While armies clashed on the beaches of Normandy and the fields of Stalingrad, a secret war was being fought in basements and forest clearings by men and women whose names never appeared in official dispatches. Twenty gripping true stories of the resistance fighters, saboteurs, and underground operatives who changed the course of World War II from the shadows.

Blown Cover: True Stories of Cold War Spies, Double Agents, and Deadly Betrayals

The Shadow Wars Series • Book Three

In the corridors of power in Washington and Moscow, the most dangerous war in history was fought without armies. Twenty true stories of the spies, double agents, and defectors whose betrayals brought the world to the edge of annihilation more than once.

———◆◇◆———

The Invisible Arsenal: True Stories of the Bombmakers, Forgers, and Craftsmen Who Armed History's Most Dangerous Spies

The Shadow Wars Series • Book Four

History remembers the spies. It forgets the people who made them possible. Twenty true stories of the chemists, engineers, tailors, and forgers who worked in secret government workshops to build the tools of covert war — and whose names never made it into the file.

———◆◇◆———

Dangerous by Design: True Stories of Women Who Lived Double Lives During the Most Dangerous Conflicts in History

The Shadow Wars Series • Book Five

They were recruited because their handlers believed women were invisible in wartime. That assumption was the greatest miscalculation the intelligence services of two world wars ever made. Twenty true stories of the women who lived double lives across WWI, WWII, and the Cold War — and changed the outcome of wars that history assigned to men.

———◆◇◆———

The L.A.U.G.H. Method

A laugh-out-loud guide for everyday adults who feel like they're barely holding it together. Equal parts humor and heart, this book reminds readers that it's okay to be imperfect, overwhelmed, and still doing just fine.

About the Author

Chuck Watson is a Minnesota-based independent author, writing across multiple genres including narrative nonfiction, mystery fiction, and self-help. Whether uncovering the hidden stories of history's most dangerous conflicts or crafting cozy mysteries set in the small, fictional Minnesota town of Caribou Cove, he brings meticulous research and compelling storytelling to every page. Dedicated to bringing overlooked stories and unforgettable characters to readers everywhere, Chuck publishes independently and on his own terms.

Shadow Armies and *Traitors, Spies, and Secret Agents* are his first works of narrative nonfiction and the opening volumes of the Shadow Wars Series — an ongoing exploration of the secret fighters, covert operations, and shadow wars that shaped the course of history. He is also the author of *The L.A.U.G.H. Method*, a humor and self-help book that blends laugh-out-loud wit with genuine grace for everyday adults navigating life's messier moments.

When he isn't writing, Chuck can be found putzing around in his workshop.

DID YOU ENJOY THIS BOOK?

If *Traitors, Spies, and Secret Agents* stuck with you — if it made you see the Civil War a little differently — I'd appreciate it if you took a moment to leave a review on your favorite book site or retailer.

That's how books like this get found. And how the people in these pages don't get forgotten.

Thanks for reading.

— Chuck Watson

Connect with Chuck:

Website: chuckwatsonauthor.com

Email: hello@chuckwatsonauthor.com

Facebook: facebook.com/chuckwatsonauthor

Instagram: @chuckwatsonauthor

TikTok: @chuckwatsonauthor